Do It
Afraid

Copyright © 2007 by Jessica Selzer

ISBN: 978-0-9739342-8-1

Published by DaySprings Publishing, Canada.

Visit us at: www.daysprings-publishing.com

To contact author, visit
http://www.do-it-afraid.com

10 9 8 7 6 5 4 3 2 1

Do It
Afraid

Jessica Selzer

Contents

DO IT AFRAID

ACKNOWLEDGMENTS

This book is to all those who lived in IH
(literally or figuratively) in 2004 - thank you.

To my editors Sarah, René, Melissa, and especially
Andrea who reminded me
that there is bravery even in writing.

Finally this is for my mom Irene, I couldn't have
accomplished half of what I did without your
continual love and support.

This novel is based on a true story.
All names have been changed for privacy.

DO IT AFRAID

Chapter 1

Starting Out

Hitting the 'Send' button on the computer screen can be just as hard as jumping off of a cliff or marching into battle. In my application for the Study Abroad program to New Zealand, I couldn't even look at the mouse, or the computer screen, and physically click the button to send the wretched thing away. I desperately tried to will my finger out of atrophy, secretly hoping that the computer would send it for me, but neither did. In the end I had to close my eyes, hold my breath, and with one finger held tentatively aloft, push the left mouse button down.

On April 23, I had my interview at the Study Abroad Office, which was nestled inside the grey carved stone Student Centre building. So there I was, marching through wind and snow, both horrendously nervous and excited. I was so completely anxious in the meeting that I over compensated by being excessively happy, so as not to let everyone know I was really about to pass out. They must have thought that I was a freak.

At least I was honest when they asked me why I wanted to go away. For some reason I didn't respond with some *BS* answer like "Oh I have always been so fascinated by the Maori culture and ecology of New Zealand" or "Egyptology is so well associated with New Zealand that it would look fantastic on my resume to study at such an esteemed university", instead I simply blurted out the truth. I told them that I was dying to move out but couldn't because of my financial situation. I told them that I was desperate for an adventure, a chance to prove to myself that I could actually do things on my own; that this program was my big chance to actually DO something with my life. To no longer be under the constant watch and wing of my single mother, as well as the scrutiny of my so-called friends as I resentfully participated in my predefined role as a person. This program was my chance to try to be me. The real me (whoever that was).

I really thought I had blown my chances to go by this ridiculous discharge of honesty and über-dorkyness. But I couldn't pretend anymore that I wasn't standing in the middle of a crowded room screaming at the top of my lungs for someone to notice me, when my own hands were covering my mouth. And yet, out of all of the applicants, I *was* one of the four interviewed for New Zealand, and only two would be chosen to go. I never thought of myself as being the cream of the crop or in the "right" group. Either way, I was told that on Thursday I'd receive an email telling me yay or nay.

And so the waiting game began.

As the gods would have it I didn't have class on Thursdays, which meant that instead of going to class and being productive, I could check my email 700 times. I was dangerously close to clinical insanity until it finally arrived at 6:20pm. When I read the subject line of the email: "Study Abroad Program" my stomach dropped and imploded. I was sure that I had been refused. They always save telling the losers until the end, and if I had gotten in, the subject line would at least say 'Congratulations' or 'yay!".

When I finally opened my letter of acceptance, you would have thought I had just won an Oscar, or that I was part of some cheesy-TV-life-drama-series. As the chorus of "I'm With You" by Avril Lavigne began to blare on the radio ("Take me by the hand, take me somewhere new" – I kid you not), I read the line of my acceptance into the program. I was speechless and had to read it again because I didn't believe that I had read it right. I must have hallucinated. But the letters and words and sentences really did mean that I was worth sending away on this chance. All I could do was put my hands to my mouth, and sob. I felt for the first time that my life was going to change. I had done something right. Everything was in slow motion but travelling too fast to understand.

Mom walked in the door a few minutes later, arms filled with groceries, Sammy bouncing and barking a big hello, and all I could say was "I got it". Of course once it started to sink in I realised that I had accomplished nothing all day, still had an essay to write, and Mom was more preoccupied with making dinner and settling the puppy than with me. She was happy for me of course, but busy. I called the Morgan family (our Framily as we call them – not family, but more than friends) as well as my dear friend Gracie, who had bid me call her once I found out.

"OH.MY GOD!!!! *squee!* Jess!!! You're going to study in Middle Earth!! Eeeee! You're going to meet an elf! Maybe Orlando Bloom!!! OOH! Maybe, you'll meet Orlando Bloom and *then* you'll *marry* him!"

Laughing at the ridiculousness of her imagination "Or not...."

"What? It could happen."

"Yeah, and I could also be spontaneously kidnapped by Ninjas that melted out of the walls."

"Well now that's just silly. Alright, maybe Frodo then? He's cute."

The next few months involved applying for Visa's, deciding on accommodation, packing, buying a laptop, and shouting at OSAP (student loan) representatives who first would and then wouldn't give me money, and then at the last minute would again but not as much of a bursary as before but now more of a loan. *Whatever.*

Journal Entry February 10th.

What am I doing? This is so dumb. This is pointless. What am I running from? Myself? Everyone else? My life? Everything. Can I even run from it? Can I be everything I want to be by leaving this all behind? What am I running to? A dream that will vanish once I get close to it? Once my tired, reaching hands touch it, will it dissolve and reveal a world that is dark and cold? Once I grasp it, will I be able to hold on? Be brave enough to take it? Take the leap of faith into the light, or is it darkness, I can't tell anymore. Who am I pretending to be? Someone brave? Someone wonderful? Won't they all be surprised when they see the real me. What do I have to offer? So much to take, to take but what to choose? What if I am making the wrong choice? What if I hate it there? What if no one there likes me? What if I become small in the shadows? Will this all be for nothing? What will I be when I get back? ...What am I now?

Dreaming about doing something is much easier than actually doing it.

February 20th I was officially and literally "leaving on a jet plane." - I spent the morning watching Disney movies and doing cross-stitch on the couch. Mom made me a salad and I started to cry because it was the wrong salad dressing.

"It's IMPORTANT MOM! They won't have this dressing there! I'm not going to have anything I'm used to for an entire year and you can't even buy the right salad dressing?!! What's wrong with you?! Don't you get it?!"

She looked at me with pain in her eyes.

"I thought you liked this dressing, we bought it last week."

"I DO like it but not NOW! My favourite is the other one!"

"Well it's too late to go to the store to buy the other one, we have to leave soon. Do you want me to make you something else?"

"No. This is fine." I pouted cross-legged on the couch.

My subconscious suddenly reminded me of a part of the "safety abroad" lecture we were all forced to go to. *Just remember that if you are standing in the middle of a supermarket one day and want to throw a tantrum because they don't sell the right kind of crackers, that it is completely normal and you are just feeling homesick. You will feel homesick before you leave, when you get there, and then reverse homesickness when you get back. Whatever you do, when you are feeling like that, don't lock yourself away, and try and talk to another foreign student about your feelings because they will understand.*

I turned on the news and caught wind of the storms that were in New Zealand at the moment. According to the news, the South Island was basically under water, and the North Island was being plagued with tornadoes and rain. The worst storm since 1908 they were saying. *Oh that's just perfect.*

When the Morgan's arrived around 1 p.m., we piled everything into their navy Buick to go for lunch at the Mandarin Restaurant. The last lunch we would all have together for a year. The restaurant was having a dumpling festival and so, (only to be respectful of the culture of course) I inhaled about 20 of them along with a few bowls of plain chicken broth.

From the restaurant to the airport the traffic was so abominable that we had to take side roads to get there on time. Meanwhile, the fact that I was about to be leaving for a year all by myself started to really sink in. I couldn't breathe and I thought I was going to throw up. Or maybe that was just the dumplings. Either way I felt like death by the time we got there, and my knees were shaking.

My first test of bravery was when the agent at the check-in desk decided that hand-written tickets were no longer accepted as of last week.

"Yes I'm sorry ma'am your travel agent should have known we only accept computer printed tickets. You'll have to rebook and come back."

OhNoSheDidn't! She can't do this to me now. Not now that I've finally gotten here. I took a deep breath.

"So what you're telling me is I have to drive back to Mississauga, call Travel Cuts, get my flight rebooked and come back, late for the start of university, because my ticket has handwriting on it?"

"Yes."

My hands were shaking, but I took strength in my family standing behind me.

"Is there somebody else I can talk to?"

It seems God was making sure that I was determined to go, and not bow out like a coward at the first opportunity. Once her manager came over, the ticket problem was rectified but I was told that my carryon was much too heavy. So I had to take out my laptop and carry it until after security where I was allowed to put it back into my suitcase. *That makes sense...*Also, there was no place for families to say goodbye to loved ones, so after the check-in fiasco I had to tearfully choke out sayonara and go straight to security. I was trying *so hard* to be strong and unperturbed by my impending adventure, but I couldn't hold it together. Mom was strong for me and held me like it was the last.

I suppose US customs and security was so easy on me because with my mascara streaked cheeks I probably looked like a basket case that could melt into a puddle of tears at any minute. The only question I had to answer from the young sandy haired officer behind the customs desk was "Don't cry, where are you going honey?". He took my pile of papers and identifications, flipped through them, wrote on a form that I was going to Auckland, Australia, (!?!?) and waved me through as another guard helped me with my luggage, I honestly feel I only made it through airport security with the help of the employees.

Besides sobbing uncontrollably, there was no way I could lift either of my checked bags onto the conveyor belt, which led into the x-ray machine. One of the guards kindly picked it up for me, and SNAP! *They broke my freaking bag!* The handle just ripped off, and the metal piece that attaches the blue strap to my bag almost hit the poor man square in the eye! Granted that did make me stop crying for a minute as I stifled a giggle at the sheer ridiculousness of the scene. *Piece-of-crap-made-in-Canada suitcase. What if this is an omen? I'm not going anymore. Wait. So where is my gate?* I called mom from a payphone, like she asked, once I calmed down and found my gate. 'Cause you know, I could have been mugged or shot or disembowelled by rabid turkeys between the check-in desk and the gate. They called our flight, we stepped onto the plane, and I agreed to swap seats with 18A because two Asian women wanted to sit together. *Whatever. As long as I get a window seat.*

◉

So when the lights and music flicker on and off before take-off that IS normal right? Right? I mean a trouble with the fuses doesn't mean that the air will get sucked out, or that the plane will stop running mid flight and crash into some south-western state splattering our guts, blood, and crushed charred bones over the prairie land as a startled and confused milk cow looks on with horror and moos a mournful...moo.

The plane turned as the safety video started. *Do cell phones really interfere with the plane that much!? So you are telling me that if I make a quick phone call in the middle of the flight that all of the high-tech-made-in-Japan airplane radars and doohickies that they spent millions of dollars on will suddenly freak out, explode, and leap out of the airplane leaving us to fly with not but a flashlight and our arms as propellers?*

The lights and music flickered again. *What the hell!? Are they restarting the airplane or something?! Dude, fix the goddamn fuse already! You're freaking me out!*

As the night and flight to Los Angeles progressed, I looked out the window towards the west and saw a sunset. A line of fire topped by a green line and then a turquoise wash into black. To the east there is nothing. No shape at all. Once the sun went down I felt like I was on a Disney Land ride and if a giant pirate ship should have floated past, I wouldn't have been surprised. The plane shuddered like we were on a rickety track and the dome around us sparkled with Christmas lights. I had been instructed to stay awake by my well-travelled Auntie Anne so I could sleep for the long haul. So I read, watched the in-flight movie "School of Rock" while laughing like an idiot (while the woman beside me watched me in bewilderment), and stared out into space.

We finally descended through the cumulous clouds, and I saw thin black shroud hang and drape itself over the orange and blue lights of Los Angeles. It was now 1am Toronto time, I was completely buggered, and I soon discovered that I hate this Airport. *What the crap is up with this place!? Do they just assume that everyone knows where to go? Why are there no signs, and the ones they do have are not in English!? Do Amerians not speak English!?* As I got off the plane, I was instructed to change terminals by going outside and taking Bus A to the Tom Bradshaw Building. *What bus??? There is no bus!!* There are cars whizzing by and a parking lot, and palm trees, *and ooh pink flowers*, but no bus, and no signs telling me which way to walk or stand. *Okay...calm down... lets go to the right.* After walking for a few minutes, I see a bus, not Bus A, but a bus going somewhere and somewhere is definitely better than here. I hop on and ask the driver if this bus would take me to the Tom Bradshaw building. He laughed at me and replied that the building is about half a block in front of me. And now there is a sign. *Of course.*

The inside of the International Terminal reminds me of a mall. A mall with armed security, and people squashed together ubiquitously. *Is it an L.A. thing to NOT line up? I mean is this difficult? Must you funnel?* I pushed my way up to the counter where they informed me that my carry-on bag, which was sort of fine in Toronto, is now too heavy and I had to check it even though my laptop was outside the suitcase. They gave me a crappy red-white-and-blue-striped plastic zip bag where I took most of my stuff out of my carry-on (so it wouldn't get stolen or broken), checked it, and carried around this crappy plastic bag with all of my crap in it. *How is this better than a suitcase? Crap.* So now I was lost in L.A. carrying my coat, a laptop, 2 plastic bags with stuff in them, and my purse. I looked like a sleep-deprived bag-lady. *Crap.*

Once I made it through security, I called Mom from a payphone like she asked me to. The second I heard her voice I started to sob uncontrollably. I could barely form words. All I wanted to do was go home. But I couldn't go home. I was trying to be someone. *I am such a basketcase.*

At 4 a.m. Toronto time we finally got to board Qantas Airlines. I was overtired, cold, and shaky. Even my skin seemed to feel clammy with travel grime. This wasn't fun anymore. I got to my skinny chair, figured out where to put my eight million bags, tried to get comfortable, and chatted a little to the cute guy beside me who should have been on the CBC TV comedy show "Talking to Americans".

"So, where you from?"

"Toronto. You?"

"Orange County. You know, like the "O.C."?"

"Oh yeah, I don't know too much about it, other than what I've seen on the T.V. show – which I'm assuming it's not like."

"Nah not really. So you're from Canada. Must be damn cold there."

"Yeah right now it is."

"No, but like all the time."

"What?"

"Like it's Canada, it's cold up there."

"Well in the winter it is... but it's pretty hot in the summer."

"How hot?"

"Well in Toronto we've gotten up to 35 degrees plus humidity."

"35!? That's cold!"

"N-no, 30 degrees Celsius."

"What's that in American?"

"Sorry, I don't know Fahrenheit... I'm guessing 90s"

"It can't get that hot."

"Sure it can. We're next door to New York."

"Are you sure? I thought Canada was always covered in snow. You know, snow, pine trees, moose..."

What, like there's a wall in the middle of Lake Ontario and anything north of that has snow?

"Really not. So... What are you going to New Zealand for?"

"Oh, I'm going on exchange to Canterbury University for a year. I'm in Engineering."

You have got to be kidding me.

I tried to sleep, but mostly I thought I was going to throw up. I spent the flight dosing in and out of an unpleasant consciousness, feeling like I was going to die. The stewardess was very kind to me, although sadly did not bump me to first class, and brought me crackers and lemon flavoured anti-nausea stuff, which worked well. In the end I am pretty sure that I got a straight two and a half hours of sleep, because all of a sudden I was perky, awake, and playing Tetris on the console on the back of the chair.

Two hours before we landed the sun was shining and breakfast was finally being served on the plane. *I can see the ocean!* As we made our final approach, the clouds took on the shape of long cylinders, like the floor of a bouncy-castle. I guess that is why New Zealand is the "Land of the Long White Cloud". *I left on a Friday, and it is now Sunday. Where did Saturday go?*

DO IT AFRAID

Chapter 2

Arrival into Middle Earth

Landing in New Zealand is like landing in the middle of a farmer's field, with palm trees. As the plane landed I could feel the warmth and humidity seeping through my window. My nose was plastered to it the entire time. My nausea was quickly replaced with the most wonderful feeling of excitement. I could barely contain myself. I was finally here.

I was graciously picked up by friends of my Aunt at the airport, but one of the first things that I noticed, besides them driving on the wrong side of the road, were these trees that look like a pine tree and a palm tree genetically smushed together. It's called an Araucaria or more commonly, a Monkey Puzzle tree, but there are no monkeys in New Zealand, nor does it look anything like a monkey, or a puzzle. Whatever, the sun is shining and the cicadas are screaming!

I arrived laden with bags to my university residence "International House" early afternoon. A blonde girl behind the desk named Leah showed me through brown brick corridors to my room and then told me of the hostel tour later on that day.

I lived in the Hobson building, room 107. My room was 4.2m by 2.4m exactly. Or so they say, I never measured it. My walls were of a light red brick, and my curtains had a Mexican feel to them, colourful and geometric. My bedspread clashed with both, and was blue, with yellow and red flowers, and geometric patterns that were completely different from those on my windows. My desk was grey and took up half the room. To turn on my light you must flick the switch DOWN. To turn off my light you flick the switch UP.

Immediately I changed into a summer blue jean halter dress, and left for the most pointless tour ever. After some banter between two R.A.'s over who would take us around, I toured with a girl who looked like she fell out of an 80's rock video, and I'm fairly certain that neither of us retained anything. All the hallways and common rooms look exactly the same. Thank God my room only involved one staircase and a hallway or I never would have found it again.

◉

At dinnertime I met a whole bunch of people from all over the world, and as the name suggests, 70% of the residents in my building are from somewhere other than here.

I did learn that not everyone knows that much about Canada. A girl from Singapore was sitting beside me and was both perplexed and fascinated that Canada was not a part of the U.S.A.

"Oh, so you're American!"

"No no. I'm Canadian."

"Yes. You are from America."

"No, I'm from Canada... We're a different country."

"What?"

"Canada and America are two separate countries. We both live on the continent of North America... But Canada has never been a part of the United States."

"Really?! So you have your own money, and government?"

"Yeah..."

"Oh I'm so sorry! I didn't know! What is the matter with the schools in Singapore?! You were really never a part of the United States of America?" *ohmygod*

I also met Louise this first night, she was originally from South Africa and for whatever reason tried to explain to me how her last name was the comparative for the word Best. She had stick straight short blond hair and dressed conservatively, but you could tell through her eyes that she had a silly sense of humour. Without blinking she stole a piece of Phil's (a blonde haired freckled kiwi boy) dessert, who happened to be sitting beside her and had made the mistake of daring her to steal someone's dessert.

"Hey WHAT?! No!!! Dammit woman, give it back!"

"No way! You asked for it."

A Korean girl named Marie threw her head back and laughed freely before grinning widely and also stealing a piece of his dessert. When he realised that this was a losing battle he changed the topic from food thievery onto me.

"So... Canada EH? Tell me something *interesting* about yourself then."

"Like what?"

"I dunno, something...(his eyes widened comically) Amazing! Something, titillating!"

"Okay... um... last month when I was walking home from the train station, I found a coconut frozen in the river."

"Really? A coconut? In Canada?"

"Uh huh!"

His eyes went squinty. "Are *you* suggesting that coconuts migrate?"

"No, a Canadian goose could have gripped it by the husk."

"Nice. Wait. Are you putting me on?"

"No, no. I literally found one. Really."

"That's brilliant!"

Louise, Marie, and I all hit it off and agreed to sit with each other again at breakfast time.

◉

Cicadas woke me up the next morning. Not the fairly quiet, polite Canadian kind, but the loud obnoxious-wake-you-up-at-7am-New-Zealand kind. I suppose it's okay though because breakfast started at 7:30 a.m.

I went shopping that day for school supplies with Vicki (California), and Abby (Te Kuiti, NZ), however managed to buy a red and black skirt in the process. I also did some basic chores like setting up a bank account and figuring out the campus. Walking back with Abby we learned that just because you speak English does not mean you can communicate.

"Hey Abby, do you mind if we pop into a convenience store on the way home? I need to grab some loonies for the laundry machine."

" *laughing* You want to go where for what?" Once she figured out what I wanted she replied with "Ah sweet as! I'm sure we can suss out a dairy up on K road that will give you some gold. I want crisps anyway." ...I rest my case.

That night was also the beginning of Orientation week for IH (International House). We piled onto a blue DOUBLE DECKER bus *(how cool is THAT!?!?)* and went off to somewhere northwest of Auckland to go bowling. I'm actually surprised that we didn't get kicked out. My team comprised of me, Abby, Vicki, and the guys from her floor, who seemed to get bored of only bowling and heavy drinking (is that a good combo in itself?) and needed to spice things up. So we got the superman dive...the football kick of the bowling ball.... Rolling two balls at once...bowling into the other lane.... you get the idea. *And why is there a bar serving heavy liquor in a bowling alley anyway???* While bowling and behaving rather silly while still giving out introductions, from the corner of my eye I spotted a boy, shorter than the rest, but rather good looking and grooving to the music that was blaring overhead. No one knew his name yet and I didn't get a chance to speak with him as he wasn't particularly loquacious or gregarious and everyone else seemed to take up my time.

DO IT AFRAID

Chapter 3

Beware Locals with Spears

The next day IH went the Waiwera Hot Pools. Waiwera in Maori literally means: Warm Water. How original. Travelling north of Auckland, once again seated at the top in the blue double-decker bus, I saw the land change so quickly it should not have been real. It went from a sheep and cow infested Hobbiton, directly to a tropical rainforest, then to flat meadows to harsh mountain cliffs. I also discovered the bottlebrush bush (say THAT ten times fast), which looks like it sounds; little leaves surrounding a bright red cylindrically shaped fuzzy flower.

The Waiwera hot pools are smack-dab in the middle of a hilly rainforest area. The pools look like normal blue chlorine swimming pools, except for the fact that they have that wonderful chemalicious smell of sulphur and chlorine. Shallow covered relaxing pools with waterfalls, uncovered pools for swimming, a spa to get a massage (which was way overpriced and as such very empty), and the most KICKASS water slides anywhere. I went on a smallish one called the Blackhole because I'm not a good swimmer, but I was sliding so fast in the dark and twistyness that I think at one point I was actually defying gravity. I had no idea what was going on and then suddenly without warning I found myself underwater with marbled sunlight above, getting a bathtub full of chlorine -sulphur water up my nose and into my lungs in the process. Yay? Needless to say I didn't go on the bigger ones as it took me quite a while to sputter and cough everything out and didn't feel the need to try it again.

That afternoon I met a newly immigrated-from-Swaziland blonde curly-haired girl named Jackie, and immediately wanted to be friends with her. She was so pretty and laughed easily. She was with her equally handsome boyfriend though, and I couldn't think of any pointless conversation topics after the usual roster of introductory questions, and she reminded me of those really cool outgoing beautiful people that I would probably never be friends with, so I let her be, and spent the rest of the day relaxing in the hot pools, with my back against the rock wall so the waterfall could massage my neck and shoulders while chatting to Louise and Marie. Or I tried to relax anyway... the boys, especially Phil, kept splashing us 'by mistake'. But not to worry, Louise fought back like a demon, attacked Phil, and was dubbed the 'bodyguard'. You just don't mess with Louise.

When we returned that night sleepy, happy and hungry, we discovered that the hostel's mission was to starve us and then give us such bad food that we would no longer be able to tell the difference. Our meals went down the drain, into the river, and washed up on a termite-infested beach. They officially stopped feeding us to the point that we were wondering if there was a Third World appreciation year no one had told us about. As a hint to the coming "meals" for dinner we had chicken and potatoes.

"Hang on I'm going to get some more gravy for my potatoes, be back."

"I thought we weren't allowed seconds!"

"Does gravy count as seconds?" all around the table were the blank stares of ignorance. I skipped up to the counter and spoke to the gray-haired woman holding the gravy ladle.

"Hey, um, could I have an extra scoop of gravy?"

She looked at me in horror and disgust,

"What? NO! You know you're not allowed second helpings! How DARE you ask me?!"

"I.. uh... I'm sorry?.... I didn't think gravy was that big of a deal... we have lots right?"

She scoffed at my suggestion and glared at me through her smudged thinly-rimmed glasses. "And what happens if I give *you* more gravy?! Then EVERYONE wants more gravy! And then there are those who wouldn't get ANY gravy all because of your greediness for gravy! Now go away!"

I slowly walked back in shock to my table and warned my friends to never ask for more gravy. Louise looked up concernedly.

"Good lord Jess, she actually yelled at you."

Phil, looked at another boy Johnny seriously and nodded, "More."

"She asked for more..."

"More?! She wanted some ... MORE?!"

"SHE asked for MORE!"

"Moooore!?! How DARE she! MORE?!!"

"Giiiirlll for saaaaleeeee..... Giiiirrrllll for saaaaleee"

Despite the foreshadowing, most of us thought that the kitchen staff's Dickens-esque outburst was an anomaly and meal times would return to normal. However, lunch the next day was an insult to the word 'food'. For lunch, we got a half-scoop of rice with a few peanuts and 4 paper-thin (sliced 1 cm wide and about 2cm long) bits of salami. They called it Nasi Risotto on the board; and I hope it wasn't an allusion to how the first word could be mispronounced...however we believe it was, especially since the food never improved in either quality or quantity.

Some of us thought that maybe if we came into the dining hall with big aluminium baseball bats with large rusted metal spikes sticking out of them, that we might seem a little more intimidating (or at least dodgy) and get either a larger portion of food, or the food would miraculously improve and gain the official ranking of "decent food". And if that didn't work, we could raise an army of hungry, nutrition deprived, International House students and arm them all with trench coats, spiked aluminium baseball bats, and large metal soup ladles (which they would hide in their sock as back up). Then, then they would fear us. Oh how they would cower in the corners. Yeah. Yeah that's the plan. You just wait, tonight the dining hall, tomorrow New Zealand, and then, and then the world.

◙

The very first week the International Centre had organized a few other orientation activities for us foreigners, and so on the morning of February 25th, I went to a traditional Maori welcome called a "Powhiri". By the time me and the Americans, Vicki, Travis, and Jenn arrived at the Marae there were at least two hundred people waiting outside, and there would have been no way for us to see what went on. Luckily, we are greedy opportunistic North Americans. Two cars had to pass through the crowd to get to wherever they were going; and since the crowd had to separate to let them pass, we took the opportunity of piggybacking on the cars' size and waltz our way to the front.

We began by waiting outside the carved red arch entrance to the Marae (the communal house (pronounced mar-eye)). Then our leader, who instructed us to be very quiet and stone faced lest the warriors should eat us, made a call. The women standing on the porch answered it in a wail and began to shake their hands with an exaggerated tremble and wide eyes. Then the Maori warriors answered it. As they grasped their carved spears, one of them shrieked and menacingly bounded towards us. Jerking one foot, then the other, closer and closer all the while screaming and making terrible contorted faces. His eyes bulged out of his head and he stuck out his tongue while emitting a vomiting noise, taunting us to fight. Then almost suddenly, he slowed, knelt down and pointed his spear to the ground, where our leader stepped towards him, through the archway, and picked up a leafy branch. The warrior sprinted away, and immediately another ran up and challenged us in the same manner.

We were honoured with three warriors that day because we were such a large group. This was actually considered a welcome, called a "taki". The purpose of a taki is to determine whether or not the visitors come in war or in peace. Luckily we came in peace and so were not slaughtered and eaten. Once all three warriors had challenged us, the women began to sing and chant, shaking their hands vigorously. We entered into the domain of the Marae and took our seats for the ceremony. We were in for a show. Or so we thought....from this point on it was the most boring thing I have ever done. Ever. Many Maori leaders approached the microphone and talked to us. About what I have no idea. It was all in Maori. For like an hour. Eventually Jenn started giggling, and whispers of confusion began to surface in the audience. I must have had three separate people ask me if I knew what he was saying. At the end a white man came up and summed up what everyone had said to us. "Study hard and don't get distracted with the opposite sex". One sentence for an hour. *What is the matter with this language?!?* I assume they said more than that, but considering they didn't come with subtitles, I will never know. Once the verbal torture had ended, the front row (not me) was invited up for a "hongi", which is a symbolic exchange of breath where the two parties touch noses. This meant that we were now a part of the family and could come into the Marae whenever we wanted to and eat the food inside.

Before we could go into the Marae we had to climb the stairs and leave our shoes on the platform. Inside there are dark reddish-brown statues of intimidating warriors and carvings on the walls and ceiling. Along the walls are ancestors from each tribe, and in the centre of the room are two totem pole-like structures. Apparently the house symbolizes a body. By the door is the head, and above the door are carvings of the god that got the three baskets of knowledge from heaven. The beams in the roof are the ribs and at the opposite end is the goddess of death all twisted and ghostlike. The room gets darker the closer you get to her. One wall is blue, which represents the sky, and the other is green, which represents the earth. I had never seen anything like that before. It was so primitive and frightening and beautiful. I was almost sad that classes were to begin in a few days and I would have to wait for a break to explore more of this country.

Cultural Differences

I quickly discovered that school is substantially easier here than at home because exams can be worth 75% of your final mark. I had so much free time it was ridiculous. I was so used to the impossible amount of daily work University of Toronto gave you, that the concept of a real social life was all but foreign to me. And so, I watched NZ Idol with Louise and Marie.

On one of those inaugural relaxation nights a sandfly bit me, and it hurt. I now believe that sandflies are the sneakiest and most evil of all insects. Somehow I was sitting on the couch in the games room, watching NZ Idol, and one bit me and then vanished into the night. I only noticed because a mosquito was in the process of having a drink. I killed the vampire bug with a curse and then noticed that I had a few other bites right beside it. "Dammit!" I said, "The dude got me like three times!" Then it started to swell up. And for the next week I had this giant, 10cm long, red itchy and painful welt on the inside of my forearm that looked like someone had beat me with a stick. *If I ever find that little bug I am going to take it, pull off its' wiggly legs and then squish it - slowly. So I can hear it scream.*

After my passionate soliloquy against sandflies, Louise and I played our usual few games of Ping-Pong.

OUR way. There are quite a few people in the residence who actually knew the proper rules and regulations of Ping-Pong, but we weren't them. We had rules like if the Ping-Pong ball bounces onto the floor, and you can manage to get it back up on to the table and over the net, it's still good. Also, the "proper" way to serve is under the leg, which is not a serve for an amateur I assure you, neither is one while facing the wall, which takes Jedi senses to aim properly. The last and most difficult of rules is that if you manage to hit the ball out the window you automatically win 50 points.

That evening, through Ping-Pong, I finally met the mysterious boy from the bowling alley. His name was Noah, and he was from Israel, but he denied that he was dancing at the alley – *lies*.

"I was not."

"Yeah you were, you were on my team. I saw you, holding a ball, by the ball giverback thing, dancing"

"Okay well maybe grooving, but not dancing."

"Same thing!"

"No."

"Whatever, you were dancing."

He tried to be one of those hard-core ping-pong players who was thoroughly annoyed with our new rules, but somehow amused with us at the same time. He eventually rolled his eyes and conceded to just making fun of our feeble attempts at the game and grinning at me with a sparkle in his eye whenever he could. He made me laugh so much that I kept missing the ball! That and I couldn't ignore him even when I tried. I'd never felt that kind of attraction before, it was like the rest of the world was trying to disappear.

◙

On February 28th, Louise and I decided to go to Dick

Smith's Electronics to get Internet cords for our computers. On our way out, we ran into Noah who had a chore to do as well, so he tagged along.

Now I don't pretend to know the exact name of the Internet cord, but I'm not stupid. When we got to the store, I immediately found an employee to speed up the process, and then Noah butted in. Initially I left it alone because I thought he was doing the guy-taking-charge thing, but when I realised that he didn't know what it was called either and he was not only confusing, but pissing off the employee, I thought that maybe I ought to take over. The salesman asked Noah if MY computer would be attached to a router. Since he clearly didn't know what that was, I stepped in and said that no it wouldn't but it would be connected to a plug in the wall that looks like a telephone jack, only bigger. In front of the employee, Noah turned to me and quietly said, "Don't call it that". *Excuse me? Whose Internet is this?* I laughed politely when the employee asked if he was my interpreter, but I was offended. Honestly, if I can manage to plan, organize, and fly all the way to New Zealand by myself to live for a year on my own, I can manage to purchase a freaking Internet cord. I really didn't want to confront him about the situation, especially if it was a cultural thing, so instead Louise lightly mentioned it at dinner in hopes of instigating a civil conversation. He got into a huff and stormed off.

Later that night while I was down in the laundry room Noah found me. I looked quickly over my shoulder at him and immediately felt electrocuted. I tried to ignore him. *He's an asshole. He has a temper and is bossy and rude and a dorkface and...*

"Jess?"

"Yeah?" I forgot what I was telling myself.

"Doing your laundry?"

"Yeah. Um hey, so, what was with the store today?

You like, took over and I felt like you thought I was stupid or something. You know I can buy an Internet cord right?"

"Yeah of course I was just helping you. You looked like you didn't know what to do when you got in."

"Oh. So you weren't trying to be mean right?"

"No of course not." He flashed a cocky smile and I forgot why I was mad at him.

"Oh, that's good."

"So um..." he looked at his feet sheepishly for a second "I ...don't know how to do... laundry."

Suddenly I laughed out loud without restraint. "What?"

"No really, I really don't know what to do."

"How is that even possible?"

"I don't know... my mother always did it."

I stifled a giggle. "You're serious."

"Okay okay stop laughing at me. Can you show me how to do it?"

"Um.. okay..."

I was still grinning at the ridiculousness of the request. How a 20-something year old guy could not know how to work a washing machine was beyond me.

"So I can get my stuff and you'll show me?"

"Sure."

"Hey, look I'm from Israel, guys just don't learn that stuff."

"Oh shut UP. I'm sure there are plenty of guys who can work a washing machine from there."

He quickly returned with a pile of clothes and I found myself lecturing on the importance of separating colours as well as showing him buttons and knobs while trying to not grin like this was the most amusing thing I had ever done in my life. When the deed was done I waved and started to walk out of the room with my clean folded laundry.

"Wait."

"What."

"Um. So... could I .. could we..." I wrinkled my brow in partial confusion, "could I take you out sometime?"

"This is your big romance tactic? Ask a girl to show you how to do laundry before asking her out?"

"Shut UP."

"Sorry, just odd timing. Um. Sure. Yeah, I'd like to go out."

His face beamed. "Okay! Good! So tomorrow night we can go for a walk or a movie or something?"

I smiled and nodded before turning my back and walking away. In my years on this planet I had never had a boyfriend. Not one. A few dates, but none of them ever worked out. I always got scared and then they got scared and then nothing happened. Ever.

DO IT AFRAID

Climbing

Noah and I started going out on night-time walks in the park where we talked about everything and nothing, held hands, and I leaned into his strong arms as we sat by a reflecting lily pond. I felt scared in the beginning, especially when his eyes gleamed when he looked into mine. I didn't know what to do, or what to say; I was afraid he would think I was some innocent dork. No guy had ever pursued me like he did. They all got scared because I was scared. Noah just seemed to know and came for me anyway. He never asked to hold my hand, he just did. He started coming into my head all the time. I seemed to need to know where he was even though I was pretending with Louise and Marie that I didn't really care.

On top of this, on March 3rd I lost my mind and managed to talk Louise and Marie into running for International Representatives with me. I had never in my entire life even considered running for a Student Council election, and I knew I ought to be nervous at being rejected, but for some reason I not only didn't care, but was genuinely excited about the prospect of running and planning International Night, the biggest night of the year since the 1960s. I just believed I could do it.

We were informed that we had to have someone on the team who had seen International Night before to be considered, and it was suggested that we speak with Jazmin, who was in IH last year. She agreed with the stipulation that she didn't have to do a lot of the work, because being in pre-med she had no time. Of course, there was no-one to run against us so it was a clean sweep, but just in case we made posters of writhing propaganda against the "other," and made speeches at dinner. We used slogans like "the other guy is so bad you don't even know who he is!" to ensure our victory.

Once we were elected and firmly sitting on the library couches during a Student Council meeting, I realised that we had no idea what we were doing. At all. The most any of us had planned was a birthday party... last year they had 40 separate acts, tonnes of international food, live music, filmed for all the world to see, and oh yes, 30 executives from the Student Accommodation Bureau were coming. We were in over our heads. We had to talk 170 international university students to get into their cultural groups, and not only rehearse, but also perform an artistic cultural act, like a dance or song, in front of a large audience, as well as cook a traditional dish for the feast. I made up some crap at the meeting that we would be having our own meeting to start discussing the plan shortly, so no-one would know about my obvious inadequacies. Then Jazmin pulled some strings and found us the video from last year's event so we could have some idea what to do.

Jazmin, Louise, Marie, and myself crammed onto my bed a few nights later with chocolate cookies to watch the video on my laptop. It was terrible. The filming was crap, the backdrop was embarrassing (I think it was meant to be a sun?), no-one was properly rehearsed, and I am pretty sure that the MC's were drunk. However, the Indian group was phenomenal, performing a highly choreographed, beautifully costumed, large-scale Bollywood dance, and so that is where we stopped the tape.

Taking a deep breath I said:

"Okay, guys.... Let's not do that. What's on the tape, let's just forget it and do our own thing."

Jazmin grinned.

"Yeah it was pretty bad hey! You didn't even see this one guy! He had these bongo drums? (she always spoke as if there were question marks at the end of each sentence) And he started to play them? Just sat on the floor. He was okay yeah, but he just kept going. And going. For like 10 minutes. Then he stopped, and we thought it was done so we started to clap? And then he started again!!! It went on for another 15 minutes, of just drumming!!!"

"Right, okay...so then we will make a rule. No-one is allowed to go on for more than 5 minutes at a time."

Marie looked confused "How will you do that?"

"We can make performance sign up sheets and have the rules there with a threat that unless okayed by one of us before, they will be cut off or something."

"We can do that?"

"Why not?"

Jazmin started to get excited "The other thing that was bad, was that the Island group, had like 12 acts, and they were good, but it was just too much! It felt like Island Night, and so many cultures didn't even bother doing something."

"Okay, then no cultural group can have more than 3 numbers and we will have to start early on harassing and hyping it up so they practice."

Louise looked up.

"Jess. This is huge, we really should delegate."

My mind quickly delegated based on personality and ability. There was NO way Marie could be trusted to do anything involved on a large-scale. She was lovely and funny, but a ditz. Whatever she did, I knew in my heart that I might have to help her on it. On the other hand, Louise could easily be counted upon and had her head on her shoulders.

"Okay. Um. Jazmin you helped choreograph that Indian dance right?"

"Yeah"

"Alright, well how about you're with me in Entertainment, like the acts and party music and stuff, 'cause I've been in stage productions so I have some idea what it should look like. Marie, since you're the art student, can you be on decorations and backdrop? And Louise, can you deal with the food? That's going to be a lot of work actually... calculating recipes and stuff. Is that okay?"

"Sounds fine."

"What kind of backdrop?"

"I dunno... why don't you do some concepts and bring 'em to me and we can figure out what's best."

"Maybe we should also have meetings every so often so we know what's going on?"

"Yeah okay, like once a month until it gets close, then once a week?"

Louise stood up "I think you should be the boss Jess."

"What?"

"The boss. It should be you."

"What? No! It's a group thing, and I don't know what I'm doing."

"I think you do, and besides, it was your idea in the first place."

"Yeah, I think so too." Said Marie.

I looked at Jazmin for some anti-boss support "Don't look at me! I'm not doing it, and they are right, we need someone at the head."

"But I-"

"Nope! Jess it is official, you are the giant boss of International Night. I hereby crown you queen. May your rule be just and scary."

"SCARY?!"

"Well yeah, I don't think it's going to be easy talking

Engineers into dancing for an audience."

Oh crap, don't they know I've never done anything like this before? What if I screw it up? There are people, those cool outgoing popular people, who usually do this stuff – I've never been in charge in my life.

Lucky for me I had quite a bit of time to panic and plan International Night, so I could actually focus on school, romance, and exploring for the time being.

◙

A few days after my IH election I woke up very sleepy from the dancing shenanigans of the night before, wolfed down a pseudo-breakfast and ran to the ferry docks with Jenn, who as usual was wearing her trademark blue jeans and her black hair in a ponytail, to catch the 9am ferry for our visit to Rangitoto. I was surprised that Noah had elected not to come. One, because the International Exchange people arranged for us to climb up a VOLCANO, two it was free, three we had really started getting along and hanging out (despite that one little electronic blip), and I thought that maybe he would want tramp up a volcano with a friend, and four because pretty much everyone was going.

Of course, because this was a Sunday it was impossible to get a packed lunch unless you prearranged it with the kitchen staff and the RAs, which we forgot to do; so we were cleverly off to climb a volcano without food. We left at quarter to nine and made the boat by seconds. At the ferry docks I quickly bought a bottle of water, however the shop sold nothing that resembled food.

Rangitoto is a Maori word meaning "blood red sky". Strangely enough, it's not about a volcanic eruption, but referencing a battle where a great commander of a war canoe was badly wounded. The ferry ride over was absolutely brilliant. The ocean was turquoise and being still early in the morning, was teeming with the sparkling reflections of sunlight. In the distance, I could see other islands blue and grey still partially hidden in the fog. The closer we got to the island the bigger it looked. The peak is at 260m and it is the highest Volcano in the Auckland area.

There were a few paths that we could have taken but we decided to take the quickest way to the summit. So like straight up. The walk only took an hour but it felt like five. I was clearly not in shape. The tramp was wonderful despite the near heart attacks we almost gave ourselves. There are fields of volcanic rock everywhere that look like rivers of freshly tilled earth and then right next to it is very dense shrubbery mixed in with ferns and palm trees. There is also ground cover that Jenn named "green tulips". She felt that they were really the best plant ever because, "I mean everyone likes green, and everyone likes tulips, so why not put 'em together, right?" Jenn was constantly making hysterical jokes about everything the whole way up which kept me both happy and dangerously out of breath.

At one point we collapsed into a heap on the road and decided that we were never going to reach the top. The signs kept telling us how many minutes to the summit were left but we never seemed to get there. Ever. We just kept going up, up, up, under the blazing sun, with no sign of food, water, or life, buzzards and hyenas circling (ok that last part didn't happen). And then in a burst of energy we collected ourselves off of the dirt path, rounded the corner just up ahead, and found the top. It was like right there. Well sort of, we had reached the crater. The crater of Rangitoto is not exactly the top; it is a look out point where you can see the crater and the forest that had grown into it. It's pretty nifty, but we had to go on. The quest for the summit was not yet over. Luckily there was a staircase and a sign right next to it. Signs make quests so much easier. So once again we climbed... up.

The view from the top is almost indescribable. You really had to be there to see it and no camera, no matter how National Geographic it is, could possibly capture it. Islands of all sorts faded into the horizon like a matte painting, and the ocean absolutely shone. Even the view of the city was wonderful. Once we were all well watered and rested (at least we had the forethought to bring water with us, and Jenn had made a peanut butter sandwich that we split – I seriously owe her for that one), we saw a bumblebee the size of a small dog, and then we tramped down to the path for the lava caves.

These caves are not well marked – actually they're not marked at all, nor the way to them, except for the occasional post with a yellow dot on it.

Going through caves without a flashlight is quite the experience. We entered the cave and were immediately plunged into total darkness. When Jenn and I realised that no-one else going through the caves seemed to have a light either, we started laughing at the sheer ludicrousness we had gotten ourselves into. To make your way, you must walk facing the wall with your hands attached to the rock, gingerly feeling the centimetres ahead with your big toe, to avoid falling over. The floor is not level and has many obstacles to trip over and holes to fall in. Pitch black, pitch black. Took a photo and blinded everyone. Found a skylight that had foliage falling into it, but once you passed the skylight you couldn't see again. Blackness, blindness. *I think I just touched a spider's web. Shelob's gonna to come out, bite me, roll me up in her web and slowly eat me alive. Where is that glass thingy Frodo had when you need it?* Darkness, darkness. The ceiling became sharply lower and lower and lower until we were crawling on all fours in the abyss. And then we saw it. We saw the opening to outside and sunshine. Exit straight ahead.

We were out.

We didn't die or get injured, and after the run down the volcano to catch the 12:45 ferry home (made an hour walk in half the time thank you very much) so we could go out for Korean food with some others from the hostel, we were positively EXHAUSTED.

When I got back to the hostel I found Noah sitting alone in a common room watching TV. I was elated about my first big adventure and wanted to tell him all about it. He smiled politely but really wasn't interested in hearing about what he missed out on. When I asked him why he decided to not come with us, he just said that he didn't feel like it. I didn't understand.

Louise and I decided to spend the rest of the evening together, in a night of spicy noodles. Let me rephrase. Louise rarely had any noodles, so she ate some of mine. Again. Unfortunately the "Malaysian Invasion" had already overrun the Common Room. This was a term coined by the entire hostel for what happened every night at midnight. Every Malaysian in the hostel would come to the common room and eat noodles. It was packed. You had to step over people to get to the microwave. So we made our noodles as quickly as possible, and headed to her room instead where I admitted the truth.

"Louise, you know I really shouldn't be the boss for International Night right?"

"What? Why not?"

"I've never done anything like this before! Like ever! What if I screw it up?"

"We won't screw it up, and besides it can't be as bad as last years."

I giggled at her allusion

"Yeah okay, but I don't want it to be average. I want it to be amazing. I want people to be like 'Whoa those girls are awesome, look at the job they did!'"

"Ah Jess you're putting so much pressure on it!"

"Yeah I know."

"What are you the most worried about?"

"Besides screwing up?"'

"Yeah."

"I guess having no one hold up their end. Like if people don't do it there IS no International Night."

"You think no one's going to listen to us?"

"I don't know. Maybe."

"Hmm."

"Okay, you're right, I'm being a dork. People WILL listen to us and it should, no, *will* be fabulous right?"

"Right! And I'll harass people, and Marie will bother people, and you will harass people so no one will forget to practice."

"Maybe we should start harassing now."

"Now? What you wanna make signs or?"

"Or have a meeting or an announcement or something. People need time to panic and think of what to do and to practice and stuff."

"Well it's sort of early, but why don't we get the RAs to hold a hostel meeting for us next week?." I nodded in agreement and felt better. "So.. what's with you and Noah? Are you going out?"

"I dunno, sorta." I lied.

"Sorta? You've been together a lot lately aye."

"Yeah, but just on walks and stuff, nothing serious."

"Do you like him?"

I smiled. "Yeah."

○

A few weeks before, I had made arrangements to meet with the brother of a family friend of ours. At 10 o'clock in the morning I got on a city bus to Onehunga to meet Gerard and his family. First I got on the wrong bus and ended up on this crazy round about way to get to where I was supposed to go, but got there unscathed, and Gerard met me at the bus stop. He seemed like a nice enough person, but then he took me to a seedy bar where I was hit on by his old, wrinkly, chain-smoking, drunk friends. Have you ever been hit on by a drunken 70-year-old man? No. I didn't think so.

"You know, I thought I could only fall in love once, but today you proved me wrong." Ew.

I was offered a beer or some other alcoholic beverage. I politely refused saying that 11am is a little early for me to begin drinking, but a cranberry juice would be nice. I think that was the funniest thing the entire bar had heard in a long time. Apparently cranberry juice is not a staple in seedy bars. Who knew? Eventually his daughter, her partner, and her four-year-old son (whose father was one of Gerard's elderly friends in the bar) arrived, and we moved into the pub next door because it was more 'family friendly'.

After a few more drinks we piled into the car (!!! *What the HELL was I thinking??*) and drove to Gerard's place where there was more chain-smoking and drinking until his house got invaded by his Maori neighbours who joined in because they thought they were invited because Gerard's wife had looked at their house from her drive-way. Great. More drunk people. Then the 70-year-old guy from the bar who had fallen in love with me arrived with a present of cranberry juice. Okay I admit technically that was sweet, but creepy.

I eventually realised that I was not having a good time and started texting Noah in an effort to either figure out how to leave or talk to someone sane. When I couldn't stand it anymore, I began to try and leave with every excuse in the book. "I have to be back for dinner or I won't get any. I'm going out tonight and I have to get ready. I promised my friend I would help her study before we all go out." But alas I was 'officially part of the family now', and I had to stay for dinner. Great. Now I couldn't even leave even though I desperately wanted to because I had no clue where I was other than a drunken man's house somewhere in Onehunga. I was kidnapped. God save me. (My mother later reminded me about cabs - loudly.) For dinner they ordered really nasty Chinese food because the dinner they were going to make didn't work out.

Before I could be driven home, Gerard had to have one last drink before he got into the car – because I mean, driving without drinking just isn't safe. But I got home, intact and semi-sane. When I told the girls my day, they laughed at me, and reminded me that the rest of the night could actually be saved because Marie, Louise, and I were going out dancing.

We got ourselves all dolled up and met with two of Louise' guy friends to find a club near the waterfront that looked promising. And for a while it was fun. We were dancing on the top floor and having a grand ol' time, until the fight broke out and I almost got pushed off of the platform and plunged to my death. Luckily, Marie saved me by grabbing my arm. We tried to find the birthday party that the twins from residence were having at a pub but couldn't, and then it started to rain and wind. Walking up Queen Street towards home, quite wet, the girls and I decide that we just wanted to go home. However, the boys didn't and so we got ditched at 1am on the middle of Queen Street.

We slowly trudged in high-heeled shoes up the massively steep hill called Wellesley Street, chilled to the bone from the horizontal rain and wind. A quarter of the way up we ran into three guys.

"Hey ladies where are you going?"

I answered quickly with a short smile "Just goin' home"

"Aw ladies, ladies, the night is young! You're not goin' home yet!"

"Yeah sorry, we are."

Marie smiled "Yup! Going home. Bye!"

"Good bye?" I noticed that two of them had moved to our rear and were very close. "No not good bye. You're gonna stay out with us tonight aren't you?"

The hairs on the back of my neck raised. I tried to look calm.

"No sorry boys, we're going home now. Sorry." I took Marie's arm and crossed the street. We walked quickly and with purpose hoping they would be discouraged.

"Oh come on ladies! Where are you going?"

Marie grabbed my arm so hard I could feel her nails digging into my skin. She shouted without looking back. "HOME!"

"Nah ladies, ladies come back here." They were following us. The big one with the gold chain around his neck jumped in front of us again with a smile.

I had no idea what to do. My mind was racing with all the things my mother had taught me. Don't walk alone at night. Walk with purpose. Go into a store if you are scared. Only there are no stores open that late on Wellesley Street. My mind started to panic as I realised my situation. I tried to keep cool on the outside. I looked at the man in front of me in the eyes and we crossed the street again.

"Woo! The ladies are crossing the street again!" One jeered.

They seemed to think it was a big joke.

"You're not scared of us are you? Come back here! Come on ladies don't make us catch you!"

"Jess..."

"Just keep going." My heart was pounding. All I could hear were their catcalls and the thud of their shoes on the slick pavement as they closed in. We tried to go faster. My mind was blank. I could hear our high heels clacking on the road and our breath quickening as we half ran up the hill. My heart was as loud as their voices and beat an uncertain rhythm. My only thought was an animal desire to keep moving. As we reached the top of the hill and saw our street I felt a wash of relief flood over my heart. We J-walked across just as the light turned green and a rush of cars inundated the streets. I stole a glance behind me and saw our three pursuers on the other side of the street. We rounded the bend in the road and then broke out into a full sprint until we could see the cheery lights of our redbrick hostel.

I'm never going out at night again.

◉

The next morning Marie and I tripped-out at the breakfast table in front of Noah and others as we laughed hysterically about our ordeal and made really inappropriate jokes about being screwed both literally and figuratively. Despite Noah's strange idiosyncrasies, like the fact that he would only eat chicken and potatoes, we had become pretty good friends, and now he watched me with a knowing eye.

That evening Noah found me in the games room:

"Come on, let's go for a walk."

I was curled up on the couch with Marie, and Louise watching NZ Idol and had no intention of ever going out at night ever again.

"No, I don't want to"

"I know. That's why you're going out."

"But I'm not. See me on the couch? I don't want to."

"I know, but you *are*. Actually, all you girls need to go out again soon, or you won't easily."

"I am... Are you bossing me?"

"Yes." And with that he came round the couch, took

my hands to lift me off the couch, led me up to my room to get my coat and out the back door.

"Look I *really* don't want to go out walking okay?" I had lost the battle.

"I know." He didn't let go.

"Are you going to let me go back inside?!"

"Nope, so relax."

"I hate you."

We took our usual route around the Domain, past the duck pond under the partially covered moon and then kept going, heading towards the cemetery, which for whatever reason was attached to it. We kept walking, passing the unconscious tramp lying against the iron barred fence holding hands as we weaved our way down the decrepit leaf covered path.

"Feeling better?"

"Yeah actually, maybe not so much now that we are in a cemetery at night."

"Well it's not like there is anyone here."

"Except the dead. And the occasional vampire."

"True. But I think we might be safe."

"What, you got some vampire-ninja-fu moves goin' on there?"

"Of course."

"You know, this is probably the worst place I could be right now?"

"Yeah?"

"Well... I'm in a cemetery, at night, alone, with a guy, in a cemetery. This rarely ends well in the movies."

"You wanna go back?"

I looked around and thought for a moment.

"...Nah, I'm kinda having fun. This seems so, rebellious." He looked amused and we kept walking through the old trees and mossy stones.

We wandered about the moonlit monuments and old trees until we reached a clearing with a hill in the middle, and sat down on the bench to enjoy the view.

"Thank you for dragging me out here tonight. Really. I dunno how long it would have taken me to go back outside."

"No problem."

I could sense that he was watching me, differently than before, and suddenly I felt nervous. I could feel my isolation on that cold bench on top of the hill and his strong presence beside me. I was so overwhelmed I started being as interested as I could in the view, and babbling about tombstones and the artsyness of the trees against the city's lights.

"Jess."

"Yeah?" I tried to say as nonchalantly as possible.

"Look at me."

"Um..." I nervously turned my head and shifted my eyes like I didn't know what was going on in an effort to not show that I was scared.

"Come here."

"Uh..." I looked at the ground again.

"Jess. It would be nice to know that I'm actually dating you and am not just your friend."

I kept staring wide-eyed at the dirt not knowing what to do. My heart pounded. I felt his hand on my chin as my head lifted and met his eyes. I felt his other hand on the back of my neck as he kissed me and my mind melted into nothing, and the city lights, clearing, and trees faded into darkness. He brushed a strand of hair that had gotten on my face and smiled before kissing me again.

DO IT AFRAID

Running About Like a Silly Person

I discovered in the morning that I not only had a boyfriend (*when did That happen?*) but that my adjacent neighbour Amy from Canada had moved out of IH because she didn't like the place or the food. I never really liked her and was not sad to see her go. She was not nice to me. I had had those condescending "what are you doing in my airspace I am so much better than you little bug" looks from the 7th grade through to the end of high school. I was not letting her make me feel bad about myself, but it was a hard go. I tried to be nice to her in hopes that she would warm up, but all I found was whenever she was around I felt a little like a loser. She could even ruin singing in the music room. IH was filled with musical talent. – actually IH could have made it's own band. I can sing classically. Amy can sing more like a rock star. She was really good actually, but she made sure that when I was singing that she took the next 4 songs and then called the music room a night for everyone.

At any rate, Meg, a very cool girl from England moved in to her room. She plays the saxophone and is fantastic with fire poi. I discovered she had moved in when I looked out my window to see flaming balls of fire being swung around in beautiful sweeping motions in the parking lot at night. Meg also became quick friends with

Jackie, who started coming to our floor every so often to play with non-flammable poi or play cards on the floor with us and munch on "bloody fantastic" dried mango.

Meg and Jackie are insane. One late evening, while we were sitting on the floor listening to "Sgt. Pepper's Lonely Hearts Club Band", Jackie decided that she wanted to go outside. Meg seconded the motion even though I protested that it was raining. I protested until I remembered that someone had screwed up the lights of the Skytower and had been lighting it up red and green quite out of season. So I got my camera, put on my coat and we headed for the foyer and the front door. On the way we ran into Phil and Jonny, who were also procrastinating from any form of studying. They asked to tag along, but not before they got some supplies. Jonny had been given a large floppy black hat from a gothic American girl, and Phil had a tiny rainbow umbrella. Once so armed, we were off for silliness, glory, photos, and rain.

The rain quite nicely stopped for us and we spent hours running up and down Queen Street playing with hats and umbrellas and having the most ridiculous photo shoot. Jonny started wearing the floppy black hat and linked arms with Phil who had ever so gracefully, propped up the little umbrella over his shoulder. All was well until people started cat calling them; and Jackie, Meg, and I died of laughter in the middle of the street.

At the major intersections on Queen St, at a red light, all four ways are stopped so pedestrians can cross anyway they like, even diagonally. At one intersection's red light, Phil and Jonny decided to race. In front of all the cars. We cheered them on as they rounded the corners until we saw the flaw in our plan. Rain. With no real umbrellas, and about 20min from the hostel, we realised that there by the docks we were going to get soaked. The water drops were the size of tennis balls and falling from all directions. There was no escape. Jackie squealed with glee and started spinning around and jumping in the puddles. Meg took a more direct approach to the puddles, by making the biggest and most serious splash that she could. I starting singing "Singing in the Rain" and danced around until Jackie joined in. The boys then ran around yelling like baboons telling random strangers that we had to go home now because we had class in the morning. We made our way back up the hill waving to the bewildered people on the streets or inside restaurants, and then had a rather damp, but deep sleep.

◙

On a very fine Saturday morning a short while later, Edward (a fellow Canadian I was recently acquainted with), Jenn, and I took a ferry over to the picturesque island of Waiheke. I had invited Noah to come along, but he was not interested. Approaching the island on the turquoise-blue waters you could make out sandy rock hills at the coast, topped with green pastures speckled with trees. We really wanted to check out the WWII trenches but discovered that without a car or tour-bus there was no way on this earth that we were going to make it out that far. Instead, we settled for good old-fashioned public transportation called the bus.

The nearest thing to do was wine tasting at Onitangi road. Waiheke Island is famous for its vineyards, and the views of them are breathtaking mixed with the meditative smell of lavender, which line the roadways. Rows of juicy dark purple grapes, nearly ready to burst and almost too heavy for the vine, stretch out as far as the eye can see, and then merge with the rolling green hills. The first and closest place we stopped at had no food. Only overpriced cheese. But the second place, Te Motu, had food and so we stayed.

However, the woman was quite snobby with us, and

initially just sat us on a bench outside the restaurant to wait for a table. I suppose she was not used to three students with backpacks and running shoes smudging the ambiance of her suit-and-tie-long-dress-with-big-floppy-white-hat-restaurant-wine-tasting world, because we were conveniently forgotten about. We eventually sat ourselves.

Our waiter was French, and the second he learned that I spoke French as well, he never spoke English again. However, Edward only understood a tiny bit of French, and poor Jenn was completely left in the dark. We ordered WAY overpriced food and shared the most delectable platter of seafood, smoked fish, calamari, garlic bread, and Caesar salad before getting up the courage to ask our waiter if we could sample some wine. Let me rephrase, I was voluntold for the job of asking our waiter if we could sample some wine. For 10$ he brought us three half full glasses of red wine of the same brand, but different years – 1997, 1998, 1999, and asked us to tell him which we preferred when he got back. We really tried our best to look cultured, and so swirled our glasses and smelled the wine like everyone else before we sipped it; whether we pulled it off or not is another story. When monsieur-waiter returned we informed him that we preferred the 1998 the best. Apparently that wine was crap and the correct answer was 1997. Oh. *shifty eyes*. *I didn't realise this was a test.*

Le Garçon then decided to educate us on the finer details of wine making – in French. Something about barrels and spices and grapes and how it tastes like leather. *Leather? Seriously?* We mostly smiled and nodded like we understood what the crap he was talking about. I at least understood the words... but not the content. Leather? Why leather? I later thought that maybe it had to do with feet and that was a code word for leather. Like in those movies in France when they squash the grapes with their feet? It's plausible... "Ah yes Monique, this cabernet has a most excellent aftertaste of feet, non?" For whatever reason, I broke into a fit of hilarity over this while Edward and Jenn stood on the white gravel path waiting for the tears to clear my eyes and make coherent sense again.

For the evening we found a quiet beach where we buried our feet and watched the sunset before heading back to IH. Before arriving home, we stopped at an "Asian" restaurant where we could get bowls of soup for 5$. There were more nutrients in that bowl of soup than I got that week in the cafeteria. When we got back we realised that the kitchen staff had all received lobotomies and had decided to make fish and chips for dinner. So we ate two dinners.

DO IT AFRAID

Chapter 7

The Questing Adventures Begin

Once the rush of essays and oral exams had finished, we had the joy of a real break. Not the so-called "Reading Week" U of T had where I actually read and wrote and had no semblance of a vacation at all, but a true break where I had nothing to do but see the world and have fun. I was crazy excited about my first adventure this trip – Black Water Rafting in the Waitomo Caves.

Luckily, I had packed the night before, which was good because I slept in and ate breakfast at the time we were supposed to leave (8am), and was welcomed by Noah tapping his watch at me when I got into the cafeteria. He had finally decided to come on a trip. The beautiful thing about IH was that it was very easy to find travel partners. The car we rented was a piece of crap, but all five of us fit (me, Louise, Marie, Noah, and Edward) with our luggage, so no worries. We eventually managed to leave, and made it to Abby's house in Te Kuiti on time, which is about a 10-minute drive from the caves. When we arrived at her house we discovered that no-one was there... at all.... not even a note...*well that's a bad sign*. So we took pictures, sat on her trampoline, and Edward found a dead sheep on a hill. We were really hoping at this point that this was in fact her house and that some random stranger wouldn't show up and shout, "Who the hell are you people, get off my trampoline!" But soon she came driving up the road and we were off.

The actual location for the Waitomo Caves is really not where you would expect caves to be until you are at its very mouth. The region is farmland dotted with farms of cows, sheep, deer (?), *and… a horde of ostriches?*

At the location, we were required to inch our way into very sexy black wetsuits. Do you know how hard it is to put on a wetsuit with footies and then on top of that put rubber boots that are considered tight enough to not fall off in the water?! Once we strapped on the very fashionable hardhats that came equipped with a headlight, we nearly collapsed onto the ground in a fit of laughter. We looked hysterical.

Off we piled onto a rusty thing they managed to call a bus for the caves. Small delay for cows blocking the road. Do you think we got to be driven up to the caves? No, that would be far too easy and commercial. Instead we found ourselves tramping, in wetsuits, helmets, and yellow rubber boots, through a pasture until we reached the edge of a … rainforest? *What the crap is THIS doing here?* You half expected to see a monkey jump out at you and steal your gumboots. Maybe these caves aren't real, and all this was actually created by Weta Workshops. It even smelled different in there. So green and dense. Very quiet and full of life. Little droplets of water hung in midair as if you could push them away with your hand to make a path.

In the middle of a farmer's cow field, near a gaggle of ostriches, in the middle of a dense rainforest, was a narrow rock opening into the dark abyss of the Waitomo caves. Inside the initial opening, were some stalactites, but mostly darkness. We walked, squeezed, and crawled our way down, down, down. You could hear water ahead, and now there was a little at our feet. I wondered if I really would see a weta, and hoped they weren't carnivorous. The water got about ½ a meter deep and my wonderful rubber boots were now filled with water. Eww. We squeezed through the tiniest shaft they could possibly find, each of us barely managing to get our inner tube through the opening, and then we found ourselves in a sort of a room and were told to sit down on the ground and turn off our headlights.

I looked up, and through the pitch saw a wash of tiny blue lights sparkling happily on the ceiling. These were glow-worms. They are the larvae of a fly that once it emerges, only lives for a day because it no longer has a mouth.

Right, lights back on and onwards to the unknown! Next stop was the Cathedral Dome, so called because of its shape and because it was positively riddled with glow-worms. Brilliantly magnificent. We pushed our way through knee-deep water that got progressively deeper until we had to use our tubes and get into formation. We heard a waterfall ahead and were instructed to turn our lights off. Ross, our leader, made an evil laugh and started to pull us forward, all the while the ceiling was covered in blue Christmas lights in a pure meditative silence and darkness. He informed us that this part of the caves is not only beautiful but has the best acoustics anywhere, and they have even been graced by the voice of an opera singer, so if anyone had a penchant for singing we were welcome for it. A man in the back of the line started singing "Row, row your boat" and Noah responded with a high-pitched barking dog. It went quickly downhill from there and soon the whole line was barking, meowing, mooing, and hooting. We settled down because Ross asked if we were all on drugs, and we kept hearing a mysterious loud bang in the distance. Ross then asked us if we were ready for danger. We shouted and screamed in affirmation, and then he asked us again if we were ready to face peril, terror, and probably certain death, and we howled in agreement.

We were then told to switch on our headlights and come forward. We had reached a very manmade railing and a waterfall that was like 7 feet high. *THAT'S the peril!?* Our job was to step up, put our tubes on our bum and fall backwards into the water. It was SO much fun! The bang was the noise of the other leader already over the falls smacking the water with a tube, ready to catch us.

Then came the hard part. We had to somehow make our way down a passage where the water was 6m deep and flowing against us. The catch is you can't swim it because your boots will come off, and there are eels so you can't have any exposed skin because they bite, so you have to cling to the rock edge with your inner tube like Spiderman, and attempt to make your way across. Do you know how impossible that is when your arms are not that strong, you can't touch the ground, the water is flowing against you, and you have long red nails so you can't really grip the wall that well anyway? At some points I managed to brace myself with my feet against the adjacent wall and kind of edge my way along, but the rest of the time I was useless and Edward had to keep pushing me ahead while laughing at my incompetence.

And then another waterfall! This one was much bigger! And outfitted with a waterslide! You got held up by one of the leaders by the inner tube, which was under your arms, over the slide and then he simply let go and you screamed your way into a massive splash at the bottom. Warning, screaming is not advised unless you want a nose full of eeled-cave water.

To get out we had to walk past crazy formations (one looked like an elephant) and then up 7 million stairs (remember my boots were still filled with water at this point, which makes them four times as heavy and make a squishy noise when I walk) to our decrepit bus. Now I must state for the record that taking off a soaked wetsuit and gumboots is substantially harder than putting them on. To take off your boots you had to hold onto the bench while two people cursed, sweated, and pulled at the boot, which had managed to become fused to your foot. After we returned our gear, we happily sat down in a kitchen wolfing complimentary toast and tomato soup to get warmed up. Well most of us. Noah, being a picky eater, bitched, and refused to eat the tomato soup even though he was cold and hungry. I just don't get that. But that was Noah; it was not uncommon to see him at the dinner table with only a couple of potatoes on his plate. Granted the food at IH stunk, but this was a level of stubbornness I had never witnessed before. We assumed that within a month or so of eating nothing but potatoes he would eventually break down and eat the crap that was given like the rest of us.

◎

Marie lived on a very nice street in Tauranga called Bethlehem Heights, in the area of Judea, (No, I'm not kidding) and her parents own a bakery, which meant that we woke up to the wonderful smell of freshly baked cheese and bacon scones. We quickly headed out to the downtown core for some fun. The streets of the core are cobblestone, lined with palm trees, and very close to the beach, which is prime for sand castle building. Our sand castle was fairly impressive for the lack of time and effort we put into it. We even tried to make a moat but by that time the tide was going out... not in... so it didn't work... Louise and Marie regressed into childhood frolicking in the waves, while the boys and I lazed in the sand. Then for some unknown reason Louise came over and asked to be thrown into the sea. Edward sat up unbelieving "Are you serious?" Yes she was, and they complied, but not very well - they managed to miss the big wave coming in, so she instead landed on the sand with the wave smashing over her. Not exactly what she had hoped for, but really funny for Marie and I to watch.

Once the sandcastle was complete and we had destroyed it by jumping on it, we waltzed a little down the road to the salt-water hot pools for some more relaxation. That was sweet! Here there were pools of different temperatures, from super hot in a whirlpool to cool enough to swim in. My favourite pool was the second hottest one that came equipped with shower heads that emitted a strong jet of water on your back and neck. I could have stayed there all day. While the girls and I were relaxing, the boys decided that they needed to time each other for how long they could hold their breath underwater. I think the longest was a minute or something.

Back at Marie's house, Vicki and her American friend Erica had arrived, and her parents had cooked us a most wonderful Korean dinner, which, to our horror, Noah did not eat. We then took the two-hour drive in the pitch dark to Ohope for the planned bonfire with Daniel, Rick, and Ben. I didn't really know them yet. They were friends of Abby and had really never talked to me before. Daniel and Rick were both tall blond and looked like they should be playing rugby, and Ben was short, Korean, and could play a mean guitar.

We had a most killer fire right on the deserted beach and we all made S'mores (the Kiwi's had never had a S'more before let alone heard of it!). The boys got far too drunk and we all had a massive sing-along with Ben on solo guitar, warmed up apples, went on firewood raids, and discovered that Noah can open a bottle of beer with his teeth. Rick decided that a skinny dipping trip would be a good idea and so I saw far too much of his bum. The rest of us sat warming by the fire bundled in our coats and hats and gloves, shaking our heads at the drunken twits in the ocean. Finally once we were all tired of gathering wood, we put out the fire, buried it, and managed to cram 11 people into a small room at Daniel's house to sleep.

Just as I started to drift off to sleep in the darkness I heard a retching sound. Sam had drunk far too much and in his sleep vomited all over the floor, his sleeping bag, and himself. The boys woke him up, took him outside, hosed him off, and started to clean up. *How is it that out of six guys none of them knew how to clean up and remove the smell?* They put talcum powder and cologne on it for God's sake! So after watching this fiasco from my warm and cozy sleeping bag I couldn't stand it anymore and took over. Poor Daniel sheepishly showed me to his kitchen with severely limited resources.

"Daniel, where are your cleaning products?"

"Um... I don't know... we kinda just moved here."

"Ok so where is the dish soap?"

"Um... I don't know..."

"Vinegar? Do you have vinegar?"

"Oh yeah we have that."

"How about baking soda?"

"I dunno... do you need that?"

I kicked the boys away and scrubbed the stains with an annoyed vigour. Marie and Louise sat in their sleeping bags shaking their heads at the whole situation.

◉

I woke up tired and really stiff from the night's adventures and lack of moving space. After a breakfast of toast and water – Daniel did not plan the food aspect of the sleepover well – we walked back down to the beach, this time in the brilliant morning sunlight and goofed off. This beach is really quite beautiful during the day, and is nearly deserted. We started off by Daniel trying to draw a perfect circle in the sand, and it went downhill from there (as we seem to do without hesitation). The rest of us joined in and started drawing randomly in the sand until we had a massive work of art, albeit a crappy one. As I looked over my shoulder I noticed that the boys were playing at killing each other and at the moment Noah and Daniel were fighting for lordship over the circle that had been drawn in the sand.

Unfortunately it was my turn to drive, so I got to drive back to Tauranga much too tired and hungry while everyone else slept except for Louise, who as my map person, kept me awake by chatting and occasionally feeding me potato chips to keep me fuelled.

The road between Tauranga and Ohope is positively stunning! For most of the way you are driving along the coast in the Bay of Plenty, with a magnificent view of the ocean, flanked by bright green, forested hills with rock cliffs; we never stopped to take photos, because it is really hard to pull over on a two-lane winding road when you are driving at 100km/hr, and besides, we really wanted to get on with the day.

We devoured lunch at Marie's and then climbed up Mt. Manganui in the afternoon. Manganui means literally 'High Mountain' in Maori, which is kind of ironic because it is not THAT high, only 230m! Well it is the highest point in Tauranga, but you won't have a heart attack climbing it. One thing about Mt. Manganui is that it is covered in sheep! The sheep were not contained behind wire, however they seemed to know to stay off the paths and in their grassy pastures. I could have taken one I was so close, but honestly what would I do with a sheep? Maybe I could make a sweater... Edward, Noah, Vicki, and Marie bolted on up the thing like they were late for tea, while Louise and I decided to take our time, and not collapse on the way up. We were tired enough as it was without running up a mountain. I think Edward wanted to go up and then right back down to get onto something else, but the rest of us were quite content sitting and chatting and looking at the view. From this height the beaches look so white against the blue waters, and if you look down the mountain, past the dense trees, (the path up was mostly under cover of trees and shrubbery) there were those crazy sheep bleating in the sunshine.

◉

Louise and Marie had stayed behind in Tauranga while the rest of us (Edward, Vicki, Marie, Erica and I) carried on to Rotorua; which smells like rotten eggs. As we entered the city, we got all excited every time we saw something smoking or fuming. Heck, here even the sewer grates smoke, and at the golf courses there are boiling mud traps so if you hit your ball in there, it disintegrates. We had to book hotels at two different places for the three days because everywhere was reserved. As we were all sitting in the 'I' centre waiting for Edward to rejoin us from his turn at paying for the hotel room, a middle-aged Kiwi man struck up a conversation with us

"Are you on vacation?"

"Yeah we are. You?"

"Yeah me and my wife are here for a few days. Where are you lot from?"

"Well we all study at the University of Auckland, but I'm from Canada, and so is our friend who's not here right now."

"We're from America! I'm from Minnesota, and Vicki is from California."

"But *you* don't look American, where are your parents from?"

"Oh, I'm Korean."

"And you? Where are you from?"

"I'm from Israel."

"Israel! No way mate! That's neat!"

"Thanks!"

"So, were you ever in the army?"

"Yes I was, for four years."

"My god, how many Palestinians have you killed?"

Oh my GOD, oh my God, please say none. Please say none. Who would even ask that? "Hi, nice to meet you, have you killed anyone lately?" We tried melting into the wall to avoid detection, but the laws of physics were against us. Luckily he handled it well "None, I was in Intelligence", and we all left as quickly as possible to avoid any other ridiculously-controversially inappropriate questions.

Our first hotel was a whole cottage with a kitchen and everything to ourselves!!! As driving, international incident avoiding, and hotel getting, had taken up most of the day, and everything closes in this country by 4pm, we only had time for one event. So we went to the Bathhouse museum. Built in 1908 in a Tudor style, we learned through creepy looking mannequins and sneaky voice-overs that an evil volcano god made Rotorua what it is, and at one point, the sulphur mud (now available at the gift shop) was used to treat arthritis and other ailments.

Then we watched the cheesiest movie ever on the history of Roturua and the bathhouse, where the wooden benches would lightly shake for added volcano effect. There wasn't any real plotline other than the educationally important timeline, but I'm pretty sure the volcano god was a red cartoon flame, and Edward made a Freudian slip during the movie calling the couple in the random and pointlessly-short-love-story-for-imaginary-plotline "cross-eyed lovers".

Because we had very little money, for dinner we ended up at Burger King, except for Noah who bought a really expensive piece of steak "to-go" at the restaurant next door, and then refused to share even a taste. When we got back to the hotel room Noah quickly plunked himself down at the kitchen table, opened his box of steak, and started cutting and eating away, while happily telling us how good it is. The rest of us sat in silence eating our hamburgers until Edward finally looked up.

"Noah I can't *believe* you actually bought a steak."

"Why? You should have too you know, it's really good."

"I'm sure it is... Um, see, the thing is, we don't HAVE $30 for a piece of meat. You could have like... shared the wealth, or at least gotten the same food as us!"

"No way! You got what you wanted; and I don't like Burger King."

"You think we were excited to eat there?"

He shrugged his shoulders, "I wanted a steak, and I'm a picky eater."

"Yeah but, come ON, are you actually going to eat that thing in front of us?"

"Yes. Yes I am."

As I slowly ate my French fries, I was also becoming irritable as Noah's steak wafted juicy temptation and resentment.

"That looks so good... Noah, can I have a bite? Just a little one?"

"No."

"Not even a little one? All I want is a taste;... I'm nice..!"

"No."

"You know it's really harsh having to sit here and watch you eat that thing."

He laughed, "I know! You could have bought one too ya know! I wasn't stopping you!"

"Noah, that thing is like 30 bucks, are you kidding me?!" He shrugged his shoulders and continued eating.

"Hey can I have one of your French fries?"

I was very annoyed, but unsure what was going on.

"Sure. Go ahead."

He took a couple of fries and went back to eating his meal. Edward looked at me in disbelief.

"Jess I can't believe you just did that. See Noah? Some people actually share with others."

"True... So, Noah can I have a piece of your steak now?"

He looked at me like I was insane and bothering him. "No..."

"What? But I just gave you some of mine!"

"So? I never said I would *trade* you fries for steak!"

Edward stared out the window. "Ohmygod you're *so* rude."

Edward stared out the window a little while longer to regain his composure, and then suddenly shrugged his shoulders, smiled and proceeded to talk us into going down to Kerosene Creek after dinner. However we didn't have a map that had this place marked, or directions to it. As well, by 9:30pm it is pitch black, and there are no lights anywhere outside of town, which makes road signs much harder to see.

We drove into the middle of a forest in the middle of nowhere to find a hot creek, after stopping at a truck-stop to ask for directions from a chain-smoked-wrinkled scraggly man with a soiled green baseball cap. At this point, the three girls were freaking out. *I have seen far too many movies to not see this coming. A werewolf or a crazy person is going to leap out of the bushes and kill us all. I am SO not walking in the pitch dark, in a forest, in the middle of nowhere to find a creek that may or may not be there. What if devil worshippers hang out there? What if we get lost?* So once we parked and the girls voiced their concerns, the boys decided that together they would go and check out the place, and we could wait in the car where it's safe.

"God Edward why don't you just say "I'll be right back"?! Don't you watch movies!? This is not a good idea."

So here's the impending plot: The boys will tramp off into the woods and then be flayed alive. Soon after a dramatically long pause of not-returning, this evil-vampire-hannibal-alien-psycho will dash out of the woods and jump onto the car bloodily slaughtering all but one who will manage to escape her wheeled-iron-alloy trap and hasten down the dirt road, flapping her arms around as all horror movie girls tend to do to convey their terror, only to be killed after a dramatic chase scene through the woods with lots of weird camera angles and thumping music. We will never be heard of again.

We were freaking ourselves out so much that we started singing "These are a Few of my Favourite Things" to take our minds off our imminent peril. Just then Tweedle-dee and Tweedle-dum came running out of the forest with their flashlight (actually Noah's cell phone which we renamed the 'SuperPhone!') making as much noise as possible. They then started screaming in an effort to scare us.

"Do they know we can see them?"

"I really hope so..."

When the boys had assured our safety, we walked down and through the thickened bush to the creek. The creek is about a foot deep and filled with hot sulphur water (which we had learned today at the Bathhouse was very good for the skin), coming fully equipped with a wide waterfall, and a rotting white sign warning swimmers not to submerge their heads in precaution of contracting Meningitis. With the stars twinkling above, the pine trees' jagged teeth darkly silhouetted our silent enclosure as we drank in the meditative stillness of the woods with the soft rhythm of the waterfall and the gentle hum of the dotted candles, which had been set into the shiny black rock face flanking us to one side.

The sand was hot lower down and Edward gave me a brilliant back massage with it, much to Noah's vexation.

However I was unconcerned with how he felt about it because compounded with his lack of sharing food, he had been basically avoiding me and had equal opportunity to sit near me in the creek. I argued later on that evening that I saw no reason to refuse a massage from a friend especially when the guy I am meant to be dating never offered. I promptly gave a massage to Marie, who then gave one to Erica, who gave one to Vicki, who in the end offered one up to Noah, who reluctantly agreed. My skin felt wonderfully soft and relaxed after, and the only downside was that we all smelled like rotten eggs.

◙

Whakarewarewa (pronounced faka-where-a-where-a) is actually traditionally written much longer, and the entire name means "The gathering place for the war parties of Wahiao". It now generally goes by the aforementioned name, and is also a substantial location for geysers, and bubbling mud pools. The only thing that stunk, besides the sulphur, was that it had been a really dry and hot couple of weeks, and so most of the mud pools were just dried and cracked circles by this point. If you go right after a rainfall there is a lot of activity then, but it was tough luck for us. Our guide was great at making plenty of bad jokes like "Hi, my name is Dave, but you can call me handsome", but I didn't retain much of the tour because there were too many people and we were at the back. The main geyser is called Pohutu, and it was constantly erupting. The foliage here is very spiky and dense and frankly we were surprised that anything could grow with all of the sulphur and boiling pools of mud.

Afterwards, we went to the free concert they offered. There was the basic threatening greeting that I had seen before, and once we were inside the Marae we were entertained with all sorts of neat dances, some with poi (balls attached to rope) some with spears, and heard a bunch of songs. I also finally saw a haka – that is their war dance, it symbolises how scary and lethal they are while simultaneously telling the enemy that they are excited to be fighting them because they will get to eat their tasty human-hides later on (*ew*). We also learned a little about Maori art. Apparently the reason why their sculptures are so grotesquely distorted is because humans were created to be perfect and it would offend the gods if they were to attempt to recreate that perfection in art.

In the evening, Edward, Erica, and I went by bus (they picked us up) to the Tamaki Hangi. This was located at a 'traditional' recreated Maori village, and for a price we were given food that was cooked in the ground (which I'm pretty sure wasn't), and a show. The bus ride there was interesting... Our bus driver MC picked an old short balding man for our war chief for our bus and we all had to practice paddling a canoe, while on the bus, to a rhythm. All the dances and songs were basically the same here as they were at Whakarewarewa, except that these ones were done a little better, but to be honest the place was kind of campy – almost Disney. Basically they had recreated an ancient Maori village with actors doing 'traditional Maori things' with cheesy props ("Ooh! Plastic meat!"). I felt like they were insulting their own culture, and we were the ignorant white tourists who came to look at the local primitives. Dinner was yummy though! I scarfed a whole lot of mussels and fish and ... fooood....

The bus ride back was incredibly funny as everyone, except for the three of us (because we had no money), was blind stinking drunk. Everyone had to get up when their country was called, go the front of the bus, while it was driving us all to our respective hotels, and sing a traditional song into the microphone. Edward and I sang

'Frère Jacques', as the cool Canadians we are! When we got to the main roundabout in the middle of the city, our bus driver asked us all to sing (and we did, complete with yeehaws) "She'll be Comin' Round the Mountain", as he drove us around it at least 5 times, with the other two buses right behind us.

Getting back to the hotel we felt a little bad that we had gone out and left Noah and Vicki to rot in front of the TV (although they had made up their own minds not to come), so we decided to find a club. Lamentably for once, we did not consult our Lonely Planet Guide and so had a very crummy night. The only place we found that had music, dancing, and no cover charge, was this terrible bar filled with old people and lesbian couples. Noah went and danced like a committed lunatic with two cougars while the four of us just stood there, pretending we didn't know him, embarrassed we were even in the place, trying hard to finish our drinks as fast as we could so we could go home. Not a brilliant end to the day, but hey, you can't win 'em all.

◉

Woke up the next morning with a distinct urge to kill Edward. Anyone who can wake up that early and be overtly super-perky should die, especially when they had been snoring like a jackhammer all night.

The boys had joyously elected to go Bungy Jumping and Zorbing. I had never even considered Bungy jumping until they mentioned it, and felt very nervous and unsure as to what I should do. Vicki and Erica vehemently declined, and Vicki had an attitude that both were somehow beneath her or that it was an activity to be frowned upon. Part of me wanted to try, I was curious, and Zorbing looked like fun. I had seen the pictures and read that it's meant to be a silly amount of fun rolling and bouncing down a hill in a clear plastic bouncy ball. Still I didn't want to go unless the girls were coming too, and they looked disinterested and annoyed. I felt afraid of making the wrong choice, as if I chose to go Zorbing that I would be bad or no longer accepted, not that I was accepted by Vicki and Erica anyway, or maybe I was but not in an all encompassing supportive friendship kind of way. The boys didn't really care whether I did or not. Edward thought I would enjoy it and tried to talk me into it. Noah asked if I wanted to, but then said that I might not be the kind of person who would like it.

When we got to the Bungy jumping station I saw that the jump was high but not unreasonably so, and there was a line-up for jumpers. The people running the station were upbeat and supportive and got the boys set up. As I watched them get ready my stomach did little flips as I considered the notion of jumping off. The boys waved at us with smiles, and we sat on a nearby picnic bench with a good view. Noah went first and we could tell as soon as the elevator went up that he was scared. His posture was different. When he reached the top I could tell that people were talking to him and you could see he was working himself up to jumping off. He must have been terrified, and rightfully so. He jumped off as ungracefully as you could, and bounced as one does before being lowered to the ground. Edward jumped next. Jumped? Nay. Dove. When the boys returned, Edward was elated and quickly told us with a grin and exaggerated hand gestures that we had seriously missed out, while Noah was sheet white and said it was 'fine'.

Finally the girls got to have some fun. We drove to the Te Ngae wooden 3d maze, in which I got lost in a labyrinth of insanity. The point was to get to the four coloured tents in the corners and make it out by the same entrance you came in by. Sounds easy but it's not. Wandering in endless circles and twists I half expected to see a skeleton laying against one of the walls with a warning scratched into the wooden slats with his bloodied fingernails "There is NO exit. Burn your way out while you still can". Up the stairs, down the stairs, round the corner, under the bridge, wait... *I was at the red tent ages ago. How did I end up on the opposite side of where I was aiming? ARGH! That's it! It's official!! There IS no green tent in the far corner. It is a myth!! There go the boys on the bridge. How did they get up onto that platform? That's where I have been trying to go for the past 10 years! The staircase to get there is blocked off! I've been around that spot for like ever! ARGH!*

"Hey Jess, are you finished yet?"

Are you telling me everyone is finished....

"No no no, I'm fine! I have to find the green tent and the exit eventually right?"

A few minutes pass:

"Jess you're in the same spot you were in like 10 minutes ago"

"WHAT!??! I am NOT!!! I must be on the other side of the maze by now."

Noah answered "We can see your feet, do you want me to come and help you?"

Well that's it then. I must be caught in a loop or something. Damn maze. Fine. I admit defeat. I suck. I have no sense of direction. I was mocked and shamed all the way to Hell's gate, and for the rest of the week.

Hell's Gate is another one of those bubbling mud/water/sulphur places. This one looks far different though and is themed around Hell, or the gate before Hell. Whatever. I think the running joke for the rest of the day, besides me lost in a maze, was around Hell. *Hell's Gate isn't so bad! I mean I wouldn't want to have a summer home here but the trees are actually quite lovely!* The basic features of Hell's Gate are smouldering rocks with yellow sulphur highlights, near dark bubbling and smoking pools of water. There are also a surprising amount of trees and shrubbery here, and with all of the smoke that raises off of the pools, it gives Hell's Gate a dark ethereal quality, which was definitely enhanced by the slow pink and purple sunset we were lucky enough to see. As usual, the boys needed to be rebellious and go off of the beaten path, even though there were numerous large signs that told you to stay on the path for your own safety. Seriously, considering that this is Hell's Gate, you would want to follow the rules in case breaking them would entice a massive demon attack. To be fair, if one of them had slipped they would have been melted. The map they gave us distinctly told us in bold print that some of the pools are actually ABOVE boiling point.

For our last dinner on our last night of our vacation we ordered Pizza, and while we were waiting Noah asked me to help him find a bag he had left in the van. Edward snorted, "What, you can't get your own bag?" but the look in Noah's eyes told me he wanted to talk. We got to the car and he quickly took out his bag from the trunk.

"So, what's going on? You're treating me like I don't exist."

"What?" Now I was annoyed

"Do you want to break up?"

I paused with uncertainty. "...no..." *Why am I saying no? This isn't going well.*

"Then why did you let Edward give you a massage?"

"Oh. My God. He offered, and where were you anyway? At the other side of the river ignoring me! You could have come over and given me one!"

"You think I liked hearing you groaning? You are the one who wanted this secret. I was staying away for you."

"Secret? What has been stopping you from hanging out with me and my friends in the hostel? It's not like we're hiding, we're in the games room. Or travelling around? You have NEVER come with me."

"That's another thing, you're always surrounded by people. How am I supposed to get you? And why do you think I came on this trip? To be with YOU. I don't care about seeing these places!"

"How do you get me? Um. Come over?! No one has banned you from talking to me in public. And what was with your crazy person dancing last night anyway? It was embarrassing."

"I don't care if you were embarrassed. But that's not the point. You're always around other people, and you're throwing other guys in my face."

"What other guys?! Edward? God, I have friends, get over it. Look. I just don't want the entire hostel knowing everything because I don't want to get teased. I've never had a boyfriend before and I don't want 170 people watching like it's a reality TV show! My girlfriends know we're going out."

"Yeah... great."

"So?"

"So I want to feel like we are actually dating. Come to me once in awhile."

"Okay..."

"Come on, they're watching from the window."

"Geez." We waved at the peering eyes at went back into the room.

After dinner I announced a room shift so I could get ONE night sleep – all the snorers in one room, and the non-snorers (Me and Noah) in another. Noah's eyes flashed in surprise. We all got ready for bed and said our good nights. I crawled into the single bed against the wall and turned to face Noah lying in the other bed across the room.

"So ... we're alone..."

"Yeah I noticed that. Good show. I just keep wondering why you did that."

I shrugged my shoulders sheepishly. "Well you said

you wanted us to be alone... so... we're alone." He crawled out of bed and knelt by mine resting his crossed arms on the edge.

"So what are you doing for International Night? Have you started thinking about it yet or," He quietly shushed by babbling by touching the side of my head.

"You're really beautiful."

"I am?"

"Yeah." He slowly leaned in and kissed me and all my blood raced to my head. His hand was now firmly on my side holding me in place, and I forgot how to think.

DO IT AFRAID

Chapter 8

Sudden Death

The rest of April passed without any major incidents. We went to school, studied, hung out and watched TV. Noah and I spent many an evening watching movies in his room and just being together; although he was a total distraction if I was trying to study. May 10th marked the start of Secret Admirers week. If you wanted to play, you had to fill out a "favourite things" form. So favourite romantic song, food, movie – some were dodgier like favourite position, room number, or body part but you could fill in what you wanted. Once they were all handed in, you received the form of someone else to admire.

Abby had someone serenading her with a guitar, roses were presented on bended knee, Marie went outside to find a giant heart made of balloons on the tennis court with 'I love you' written in Korean with candles, and so it continued to madness all week. Everyone ended up being messengers at some point.

The winning gag definitely was played on Louise. First of all, the dorkons ruined the initial surprise when they set off the door alarm trying to get onto her floor. There were a lot of them, as it was a team effort, and later they hired themselves out to other people for this week. So once they got themselves sorted and had the door alarm turned off, Louise had a knocking at her door. She opened the door and found a large cardboard box sitting there with the lunatic team, and most of her hallway, standing around watching – with the camcorder running of course. Suddenly the top of the box flew off and there was Adrian, in nothing but white undies, a top hat, and a tie, posing with one knee and a bent elbow, (*blank stare from Louise*) and he said " I couldn't help but notice your radiant beauty" (what she wrote as her favourite pick-up line) and then he grabbed his box and ran away, diving head first into the washroom.

I was surprised that not only did Noah not participate in Secret Admirer's week, but he also didn't give me anything. Not even a piece of chocolate.

◉

Noah started to change, or maybe I just started noticing, it got to the point that no-one knew what mood he would be in, he was rarely normal anymore. One day he was beyond hyper like he was trying to prove to the world that he was happy and fine, and the next the blinds were drawn, lights off, and he cut himself off from everyone only to come out at dinnertime with a sour look on his face to quietly eat a plate of plain potatoes. He started shouting at people for the littlest things or jokes directed at him. Everyone was noticing. He even seemed jealous when I went out without him, even though I had invited him and he didn't want to come. I started feeling like I was going down to his room out of obligation and I was almost embarrassed that we were going out at all. It wasn't good.

I thought that the Pimps and Porn Stars party might be fun for us though. As the title suggests, everyone dressed up accordingly and then went down to the Waterfront club for a night of revelry and phrases like "Oh honey, you can't afford me", and "She's *my* bitch, and none y'all can have her!" Granted my dress was not as whorish as it could have been, but even though I strangely didn't want to go, I made an effort and then went down to Noah's room to see if he was ready. He was in a bit of a mood, but passionately kissed me anyway. The kiss was strange, it felt forced and empty, something was wrong, really wrong, but I pretended I didn't notice and we left for the party.

Where he ignored me the entire time. Even when I asked, he refused to dance with me and just sat in a corner looking sullen. I couldn't figure it out. Here is your so-called girlfriend, dressed as gothic-porn-star as she could manage, and you won't even dance with her?!?! I must have danced with everyone and their cousin, but not him. I finally got angry and danced a little inappropriately with Cory right in front of him with the decision that I was going to break up with him. He was just not acting like a normal human being, and also, for the past week I had woken up with the same thought in my head – *he is going to break up with you.* To avoid dealing with anything that night, I escaped to the safety of my room and fell asleep with full intention of breaking up the next day.

At 8am I heard a knocking at my door. It was Noah. *Oh my God, if he is mad about Cory, I am going to let him have it.*

"Can I come in? I need to talk to you."

"Sure. *yawn* What's up?"

"Okay, you need to listen to me carefully. Wake up."

"I'm awake. It's early. What."

"Okay, there is something only 3 other people in the world know. Before I tell you, you have to promise never to tell anyone ever."

"Alright..." I said with a look of irritated confusion

"This is serious. Say you promise."

"I promise." *What am I even promising to? Jesus, did you kill someone?*

" Remember how I told you I have a psychiatrist that I talk to? Well I have a psychiatrist because I suffer from severe clinical depression. I am on medication for it. Awhile back I tried to commit suicide by taking sleeping pills. It was a cry for help. I am not capable of having a long-term relationship. I feel empty inside. All the time. Nothing. I have nothing to give you. Believe me if I could be with anyone, it would be you, but I promised not to hurt you, so I am breaking it off before I fall in love and make it worse."

I honestly had nothing to say as I stared at the brick wall.

"Don't you care?"

"I care... but I understand... You had to tell me this at 8 o'clock in the morning?"

"I've been at your door since 6 listening for you. I couldn't sleep. I never sleep. It's not like I thought this would happen, it comes in waves, and I was okay for awhile."

"Well...Alright."

"I'm sorry Jessica, I really am. If you want to talk to me about it or anything, just, you know. I'm there." His eyes got serious and his tone sharp "But you must Never, Never, tell anyone what I just told you about myself. Nothing."

"Okay. I suppose I ought to get dressed and go for breakfast now, so..."

"I'll talk to you later okay?"

"...This is insane... I knew something like this was going to happen, I just knew it! God, I'm so stupid!"

Once I woke up and the whole thing sunk in, I was devastated. Not just for losing him (whatever I had left), but for being so stupid. *So did he decide before or after he took my shirt off last night to break up with me? I am such an idiot.* The worst part was even though he was screwed up, I really did like him, and I had stupidly trusted him with a small piece of my heart. *I want to go home.* And now I wasn't allowed to tell anyone. So I called my mom and then Louise – screw Noah, I needed to talk to someone who wasn't on medication.

◉

I think the reason I was faring at all was because I had made myself very busy. The International Reps and I now had the basic layout for the evening, had commenced talks with the Chef and Hostel Manager, knew our budget, and would begin hardcore planning, harassing, and creating once the Inter Semester break was over. As well, I had tonnes of friends surrounding me, exams were near, I wrote a scathing email to Noah once I was able to collect my thoughts, and he hid in his room for the next two months wallowing in his dark depression. It was only at night that I felt the hole in my stomach.

Ironically for my final German oral presentation our group decided to translate and abridge Romeo and Juliet, with me as Juliet herself. Translating Shakespeare into German is completely impossible for a first semester first year German student, so I didn't even bother trying. Instead, I wrote out the main plot in English, some of the classic lines that *had* to be there, cut out all the unnecessary characters and scenes, and then wrote out the script, in extraordinarily simple German, riddled with bad jokes that I knew the class could understand.

The party scene was hysterically cut down to Juliet dancing to German clubbing music, Romeo walking up to her, saying "Ich brauche dich!! (I need you!), forcing her (me) into an overly dramatic über-dip kiss, and then Juliet's famed line of (*dazed smile and gasp*) "Du kuss bei das Buch!" (You kiss by the book!). Next scene, on with the show. Juliet's balcony scene had dimmed lighting and Tammy playing the violin softly off to the side while I had my speech. We noticed that in German, the word for moon sounds almost exactly like the word for mouth (Mond vs Mund), and since we hadn't learned the word for moon yet, swearing by it might not work out as we had planned, and I SO was not kissing Sascha to make it work. Instead, we rewrote it with the vocabulary we knew, and Sascha swore his love to me "bei dem Lampe" instead, while pointing to one of the overhead fluorescent lights. We also thought that instead of trying to have proper costumes and props and failing miserably that we would just... not have any... so instead of swords, we used pens, and changed all the words for sword, to pen (Oh glucklich Bleistift!) and threw in the line "the pen is mightier than the sword" right in the beginning to seal the deal. We also solved the problem of too many characters and not enough players by hanging paper name signs round our necks. The class and teacher LOVED it and nearly fell over laughing.

The rest of my exams went off without a hitch. I found that even though the exams were worth 75% of your final grade that they were actually easier than the ones I had been doing in Toronto! The two weeks of exams we had no classes, and so spent entire days locked in our bedrooms studying like mad people until we literally went insane and did very silly things in the corridors. At night the hostel provided "Supper" which is different from "Tea". Tea is held at dinnertime and probably doesn't involve any tea, only a full meal. Supper involves tea but there is no meal, only cookies or sweet breads. Either way it gave us that extra boost of sugar and quick break of silliness needed to study for an extra few hours. *God I can't wait until my South Island trip next week.*

Chapter 9

Road Trip Extravaganza

Marie, Edward, and Vicki, and I had planned to drive to Wellington in one day, before taking the ferry over to the South Island and spending the next week driving and adventuring in the South Island.

The road to Wellington is a long one. The emerald hills cascaded and folded into each other while black trees fell into their creases. Some hills have been sliced in half revealing a pale bone rock. Today the fog was as thick as cloud. It smothered the tops of the hills and caressed the bases intertwining with the trees, and slithered over the lakes.

At Tirau, we stopped for a bathroom break. Tirau is a small town with an obsession for giant corrugated tin sculptures. The town centre has a building in the shape of a white sheep and another as a white dog. Very odd.

Later on, in the middle of nowhere we came across a town of 147 people whose sole attraction was a cookie airplane. We HAD to stop. It's literally an airplane that is decorated in cookie pictures and is a cookie café! You go in and buy warm cookies! In an airplane! Okay this probably doesn't sound all that exciting, but for those who are on a 9hr drive it's great. Apparently a bunch of the Lord of the Rings cast stopped there as well for a cookie. A rather large coincidence considering this town is literally in the middle of the middle of nowhere and Marie said, "*Ooh! A cookie airplane! Stop!*".

Then the fog thickened and it started to rain. We couldn't see and our windshield wipers sounded like a tortured hamster. The dense black pine trees suddenly stopped and we were on the 'Great Desert Road'. Not that there is sand here. It was more like the 'Great Dead Shrubbery Road'. It was very flat and beige with dark red stick like plants that protruded every so often. It just looked – dead; especially with the fog. The fog lifted slightly and we saw snow capped mountains painted into the sky. Then it was very dark and rained, so I don't know what the scenery looked like the rest of the way to Wellington.

We arrived in Wellington in the pouring rain and scoped out backpacker hostels. Wellington is filled with one-way streets that are extraordinarily frustrating when you first arrive, tired and cranky, in the dark, and you can't read the map anymore. There were SO many hostels to choose from but none of them would guarantee us a private room. In the end we ended up at the X Base and were lucky enough to get our own room of 3 bunk beds. Not bad. Outside you could hear the base booming from the pub down beneath the hostel and a girl who preaching something about our impending doom in the street.

◉

We woke up very early and ate breakfast at the hostel. For $2.50 I got two sausages and a pile of eggs. Yay to cheap backpacker hostels! They understand that we have no money! The first stop was the airport - at my request. We must have looked like such geeks. Marie and I ran into the airport to ask the customer service woman from where Gollum could be seen. She looked as if dorky 'Ringers' had asked her that question 1200 times already that morning and nonchalantly pointed us to gate 17. The statue was gynormous! The craftsmanship was extraordinary, it really looked like a monstrous Gollum had broken through the airport roof and was carefully reaching towards the One Ring. Edward and Vicki were too cool to come with us until we came bounding and beaming, then they had to see it too.

Afterwards we saw Parliament, and then found the cable car to Kelburn and the Botanical Gardens where we stopped for lunch on top of a very windy hill with a human sundial near the star observatory. We spent lunch hanging on to our hats, (this is an extraordinarily windy city due to the Cook Straits) and standing every so often to see what time it was. The walk through the gardens was nice, although because it was winter most of the flowers had gone. On the way down, we found a children's playground and, because we were very mature adults, played around on the flying fox until some real children arrived, and stared at us.

We then walked back to the city centre through the shops, café's, and millions of music stores to the Te Papa museum. By this time we were all exhausted, but because we only had one day to see the city, we crammed in everything that we could. The museum was quite nice, and very big. But our feet hurt and so we didn't want to spend too much time in there. Besides the Maori artefacts, and the exhibit on Indian marriage, there was a really strange modern art exhibit with lots of colourful plastic things glued together to make odd, apparently-meaningful, slightly-disturbing pieces of "art". Such as the fertility mirror, which was a mirror, with glued on penises, hearts, flowers, and naked dolls...

For dinner we decided to be cultured and order two pizzas from Dominos. On the way back from getting the pizza, I noticed the Embassy Theatre was right outside our hostel! That was where the Return of the King premiere was! It is such a beautiful movie theatre! It had been renovated with twin marble staircases, huge gilded mirrors, and white banisters. Out of sheer principle, we all wanted to see a movie and see what the theatre itself looked like, but they were only playing Harry Potter, and we had already seen it, so we couldn't justify paying for movie tickets to look inside the door. Instead we ate pizza on the floor of our hostel and listened to the bass of the pub beneath us. Soon, Edward and his insane amount of energy tried to get us to go to the pub for a drink and a dance.

"Wanna go to the pub?"

Vicki responded first "Not really... I'm pretty tired"

"Yeah me too Edward, I don't think I wanna go either."

"But they gave us free drink coupons Jess, we *Have* to go!"

"Yeah I know, sorry, I just really don't care tonight. I'm way too tired."

"Jess, come ON! I'll even buy you girls a drink. Marie!?"

"Ack! Nooo! Leave me out of this! Go away! Take Vicki!"

"Vicki, I am begging you. Just come down and see what it's like!!!"

sigh "Fine. Whatever. Let's just go and get back."

I never even heard them come back in.

◎

I woke up much too early the next morning to catch the early ferry to Picton, on the South Island. It was dreadfully cold, windy, and three hours long, but absolutely stunning. Everyone but Marie and myself stayed below where it was warm. Once we were warm enough, we would run up on deck like lunatics to take photos of the bright blue skies, sparkling water, and dark green hills leaving Wellington, and then the overture to the magnificence of the South Island – blue snow-capped mountains hazy in the distance. Vicki got motion sickness and was so drugged up that I'm not sure she even remembered the ride over. The way into Picton was through a myriad of peninsulas and small islands that were dark green covered in small yellow flowers.

This part of the South Island has a lot of mountains and green valleys. We decided to take the more scenic route and found ourselves on the world's most long and winding road. The sharpest turns are of course placed on the edge of a cliff without a barrier, so it took us twice as long to get to Nelson because you couldn't ever go past 60km/h without the danger of driving off the road.

We arrived in Nelson around 3pm already tired from the voyage, and got lost going to Louise's house because no-one in the car could read Louise's map properly and I was instructed to turn down the wrong road. Once we came in and said hi, Louise got us all to tramp up the local hills, the Grampians (392 meters in elevation), while it was still light outside. It was strange to go from plains, pine trees and shrubbery into rainforest, but I was learning to expect the unexpected in New Zealand. We made it to the top just in time for a blood red sunset and a beautiful view of Nelson.

Only I was going to stay at Louise's house because her mom had made arrangements for everyone else to stay with the neighbours'. Actually I was glad of the separation for once. For dinner I had a traditional South African dinner. I don't know what it was called but it involved a lovely meat dish topped with egg. The night was spent relaxing and having Louise's younger sisters ask me 500 questions about whether Canada was 'cool' or not.

Up and out the door by 9am for an all day trek in the Abel Tasman National Park. Louise had to work and couldn't come with us, but made me a sandwich instead to make up for it. We all met up and I quickly learned that Edward and Marie had been relegated to some shack behind the house and had frozen during the night. On the way I found the BEST road sign ever; it's an exclamation mark. I suppose it meant, "watch out", but seems like a pretty lazy system of signage if you ask me. Most of the time there weren't even words beneath it to tell you what to watch out for, so it could have be anything! Watch out for trolls? Be specific!!! I half expected to see a question mark sign meaning, "We've got no idea what's past this turn. Good luck."

There is no way we could have seen the whole of Abel Tasman Park unless we spent a month. The park is huge and we barely covered a toenail clipping of it. The tide was low and the beaches were riddled with zagged lines from the receded water. Our trail started off in a marshland, and then we walked into a path surrounded by dense thorny bushes that had yellow flowers on them, from there on was rainforest. We walked the path nearest to the coastline, saw a few waterfalls, and were followed by Fantail birds. Frankly they ought to be called "little brown fluffballs on caffeine" They look like a dark version of a sparrow with a tail in the shape of a fan, but follow you along the path and zip round you for God knows what reason looking like they don't know where they are going with their little motors about to internally combust from being over revved.

"Is that bird still following us?"

We tried to feed them some of my sunflower seeds but they wouldn't touch them.

"What bird doesn't like seeds?" Marie summed it up "Ah. That bird is just crazy." I learned later that they were following us because they were after the tiny insects on the ground that we disturbed as we walked.

We made it to Coquille Bay for lunch and then decided to take a different route back: right on the beach. You would think that this would be a very easy thing to accomplish, waltzing over the sand, waves crashing. But this is New Zealand, so we ended up scrambling and climbing over giant fossiled rocks the whole way back, while noticing that the tide was actually coming IN.

◎

The following day's mission was to get to Okarito to sleep the night, before climbing Fox Glacier the next day. Our first stop was Lake Rotuiti, which is in the Nelson Lakes area and apparently infested with sand flies, and ducks. Marie was crouched down at the lake's edge, snapping pictures of ducks, as we watched the water barely lapping the pebbled shore, and reflecting the snow -capped mountain flanked by two deciduous covered foothills.

Just as we were pulling out and smashing the 500 sandflies that had gotten into the car, seats, windows, and roof, Edward and I remembered something very important. At nearly the same time we turned to each other and with a grin yelled *"HAPPY CANADA DAY!!!"*. Vicki gawked at us, and Marie grinned, clapped her hands and cried "Oh! You are so CUTE! Happy Canada Day! Yay!"

We drove forever. This was another one of those 9-hour drives. We were so high in altitude that clouds snaked around the trees. We drove through forest and more forest and more forest and hills and more hills and trees until we finally burst out onto the west coast where dark green trees teetering on their edges exploded out of the high jagged cliffs next to the highway and sandy beaches. We stopped at Punakaiki to see the famous Pancake Rocks, which look like, well pancakes.

This trip was quickly turning into the Amazing Race: screech on the brakes, summersault out of the car window, race to the viewpoint, click a few pictures, race back to the car and speed off to the next destination.

Along one particular stretch of highway, Marie saw a lump of fur and yelled "Edward! Stop! *Look!*"

"Marie, what?" Marie grabbed her camera, jumped out of the car, and bounced over to the small mass of fur lying on the roadside.

"Marie what are you doing?" She squatted down and turned to look back

"Look! It's so CUTE!"

Oh my god it's dead possum.

"Marie it's dead! That's gross! Come back!" She didn't, but flattened herself onto the road to get a better view.

"One minute! I want a picture!"

"Oh COME ON. *Marie?!*" With a satisfied smile she got up and bounced back to the car.

"So Sweeet!"

"Marie what is the matter with you, it's Road Kill! I can't *believe* you just took a picture of a dead possum! That is SO gross!!!"

"No! Cute! Do you want to see my picture?"

Oh look, its tongue has flopped out of his mouth and onto the pavement.

◉

We had decided to bunk at Okarito, as we had read it is a beautiful lagoon and migratory place for White Heron, however I am certain that the name was chosen to sound like a Japanese horror film. Once the sun sets there is no hope of light. We missed the turnoff three times, while a dense fog rolled in until we finally found the hidden road to Okarito. At the side of the narrow gravel road, we found a yellow kiwi bird crossing sign. Some-one had scraped a smile onto the kiwi bird, and for what-ever childhood issues that plague Edward, he was dis-turbed by it.

"I dunno, it's just Wrong! You guys don't find that creepy?"

We couldn't find accommodation anywhere, not even in the student hostel, which was actually an old school house with floor space. There was one hotel that appar-ently had space, but as we drove up the dark and fog cov-ered driveway, we saw that it was an old house. Edward and I got out of the car only to find that the door was unlocked and no one inside. No matter how much we knocked or called, no one came. Suddenly a golden re-triever slunk round the corner and started whining with huge pleading eyes. We decided to leave, but the dog would cut us off and whimper, as if it was trying to tell us something. It was clearly upset. We made our way back to the car but the dog, gold fur reflecting off our headlights tried to come too. This dog wanted us to take it with us. We had to physically get it out of the car, and hold it back as we closed the door and drove away.

◉

The next town over was Franz Joseph, home to its own glacier. We found a place instantly at the Chateau Franz Backpackers, and the manager told us that there was no point in driving all the way to Fox Glacier because Franz Joseph was far superior, and he could book us a climb in the morning. "Why do you want to go to Fox so much mate?" Marie then pulled out her trusty Lonely Planet guide and showed a really cool picture of two peo-ple in an oblong ice cave.

"You mean like *This* picture? Yeah. Oi, also when you check out in the morning, you can leave your car in the lot and feel free to use the showers and have some of my homemade soup up in the kitchen when you get back. A warm soup will do you good after all that ice."

We got a cabin called "The Stables" which fittingly had a cowboy theme, complete with horseshoes on the walls, saddles hanging from the ceiling, and black and white photos of pioneer glacier climbers. I was baffled how the women in long flowing skirts, and fancy hats could have even gotten up there, but comforted by the thought that if those girls could do it, so could I. Soon we heard a rap at our door and found our friendly hostel owner bearing a gift of a space heater because it was so cold outside and the stables didn't have central heating. We thanked him profusely as he set it up, plugged it in, and then left us for the evening. However not an hour later, Marie tripped over the half a meter of cord coming out from the wall, knocked over the space heater, and broke it. We couldn't bear waking him up and admitting we had broken the space heater, so we bundled up and fell asleep watching our breath.

DO IT AFRAID

*International House,
University of Auckland, North Island*

Mt. Ruapehu, North Island

Franz Joseph Glacier, South Island

Franz Joseph Glacier, South Island

Deer Park Heights, South Island

Deer Park Heights, South Island

Wairaka of the Rock, Whakatane, North Island

Canterbury Plains, South Island

DO IT AFRAID

Paparoa National Park, South Island

Punakaiki Pancake Rocks, South Island

Pohutu Geyser, Whakarewarewa, North Island

Boiling Pool, Whakarewarewa, North Island

Maori Art, Whakarewarewa, North Island

Daring Adventures for the Adventurers

We had to wake up at 6am to book our glacier hike, and when we arrived at the centre, which was just down the road and around the corner, we all signed 'in the event of death/maiming we are not responsible' waivers, and were given snazzy blue rain jackets, the world's heaviest leather boots, steel talons, woolly mittens, and an ice pick. I looked ready to go.

Climbing Franz Joseph Glacier in the rain for 8 hours is hard work – but utterly spectacular. At the glacier we were separated into three groups according to our physical ability. There was the slow or 'National Geographic' group as the guides called it, the medium group, which Marie, and I flung ourselves into, and then the super athletic fast group, which Edward elected to be in, which we didn't understand. Apparently he thought that the fast group was the better group and he didn't want to be held back. I half jokingly shouted

"Fine. Don't be with us. See if we care." and then Marie quipped, "Ahh, we'll have more fun without him anyway." Initially nearly everyone chose to go with this really hot leader, leaving Mike, whom we chose, in the dirt.

"What, No One wants to go with ME?! Just because I'm not as good-looking as Paul doesn't mean that we won't have just as a good of a time you know! In fact, we'll have a better time, because HE is no fun! Cooome with meeeee, coooome with meeeee."

It was a two-kilometre walk to the face of the glacier, and then we climbed through the yellow ropes and past all the 'Caution Extreme Danger' signs that had stick men being crushed by avalanches.

"Marie we're going to die aren't we?"

"Don't worry Jess I will save you!"

The first haul up was the worst. It was a staircase of death. We climbed a sketchy "staircase", which had been hewn into the rock, for more than an hour. By the time we reached the ice, I thought I was going to collapse into a heap of heart attacks and muscle spasms, throw up, and then have an untimely death - all at the same time. We were allowed a short rest while we were instructed to lash the steel talons to the bottom of our boots. Baby toe, under, big toe, pull as hard as humanly possible. Next foot.

Onwards to ice and glory!

We then climbed, mostly up, for another 6 hours through labyrinths of blue ice, pointed miniature mountains, tunnels, and crevasses. I am pretty sure that going through the crevasses was a bad idea.

"I'm stuck! Um, guys, how do you get through?"

"I don't know I'm stuck too!"

"Me too! I can't move!"

"Where's our guide?"

"He's up at the front. Gone."

"He's got to notice us."

"I wouldn't count on it, I think we're going to have to figure this out ourselves."

I wriggled and grunted but couldn't move an inch. It was too slippery to use my hands, the ice was an inch from my face, and my bag was frozen to the wall. The only thing I could move was my left arm, because I was at the front of our group. I took my pick, reached as far as I could, and slammed it into the ice with what force my wrist could muster. It stuck. I tightened my grip and slowly hauled myself half a foot forward. Again. Again. My wrist stung with every hit. Again. Again. It seemed like an eternity in the frozen corridor, until finally it widened and we were out.

A few feet later, we caught up with out leader who had brought us to a cave. It was a very small cave. To get through it you sat down at the mouth, and slid down at a super human speed until your feet smashed into the ice bottom like a wedge. Once I had un-wedged my feet from its grasp, I found myself lying on my back, wet, with ice about 15 cm from my face, my feet precariously balanced over the gap, and wondering how in the world I was going to get out. I spidered my way to the exit, which I really couldn't see anyway because of Marie in front, and we couldn't turn back because of the people behind.

"Marie! We're going to die here! We're going to get stuck and never get out again! Archaeologists will find us thousands of years later and wonder what the *hell* we were doing!"

Marie burst into laughter "Nooo!!!"

The higher we climbed, the more brilliant ice sculptures we encountered. Sometimes to cross a fissure in the ice, there was something they somehow managed to call a bridge that had been erected over it. This was more like a metal ladder, with a piece of wood placed on top, which had been mounted in the ice by means of metal spikes. On one of the bridges I actually watched our guide take out the spikes and hammer them back in before we crossed. There was a narrow rope on either side that you could hold, but in all honesty, if you should slip, that would be the end of you.

"Okay guys pay attention. One person at a time. Hold the ropes. Move slowly but don't stop for anything, - no pictures, no waving, no nothing. Do not start, I repeat do NOT start crossing until the last person is off of the bridge. Oh yeah, if you happen to fall, make sure that you land on your head so we can get the boots and talons back."

The fissures that these bridges covered were more than 50m deep, and had dark grey blue shadows hovering below. We found hell, and it had frozen over.

The grey woollen mittens they had given us were in a perpetual state of dripping wet. Because it had started to rain, (this is what's called a Warm Glacier) and because everywhere was ice, you always had damp, dripping hands. Whenever I had a chance I would take them off, squeeze them out, and continue up the ice with nasty damp wool clamming up my skin.

We stopped for lunch at what looked like a quarry. The problem with lunch is that you really can't eat or drink what you would like, because there are no washrooms on a glacier, and we still had hours to go. But rest and food were welcome and we were so high it was beautiful as the sun broke through the clouds into soft rays in the distance. Once we continued on we were lost in a labyrinth of ice, locked between two deep green rock cliffs with waterfalls towering over us.

Half way through the quest we climbed a wall of ice where I had to lift my foot past my elbow to get up. 10m up the wall we were stopped from someone having problems at the top, and I had to use my pick to keep myself from falling into the deep fissure below. As I looked down I could see the narrow ledge from where we started, and a deep blue crevice. Suddenly Marie, who was just above of me, loses balance and falls backwards. Within seconds I managed to hold onto my ice pick with one hand, catch her with the other, and push her back up until she could regain her grip.

" *gasp* Thank you for grabbing my ass!" *Jesus.*

After Marie's strangely anticlimactic near plummet to the centre of the earth, we had to slip through a very long and narrow crevasse that had a river running through it, which was at times over your head in depth. It is interesting how when there is no-one around to help you that you become stronger and more agile to push through. Our guide was way ahead again, no-one knew how to get through without falling in, and yet somehow I still managed to straddle-climb over the river using the slippery blue walls, finding some kind of tiny platforms to move along. Marie fell in. Waist deep. Four hours to go and she is soaked. We formed a bit of a team and used our pick as a water depth gauge.

"Okay guys, right here is super deep, but I think this spot's okay to stand on. Maybe"

"Where the hell is our guide? Shouldn't HE be telling us this stuff?"

We climbed higher still into an azure fortress, scuttling through tunnels until we had to loop back down.

The trip down was harder than the trip up, and the ice was still very slippery, so every step was a smash of your talon into the ice to get hold of what was left of any grip. Funny, because I was actually kind-of excited to go downhill, but the *Yay Down! I love down!* Is quickly smothered by *My legs feel like jelly and I think I might fall down the glacier! I hate down.* The walk back to the bus felt even longer.

Marie started the complaining, "There IS no bus! They have left us! Gaaah"

"Oh *gasp* My *gasp* God, I think my legs are going to fall off." I whined.

And then someone from behind shut us down "Oh Shut UP the bus is close".

After we returned our gear and declined an invite to go dancing at a pub with our guide, we got back to the hotel and discovered that Edward had got back before us, and already checked us out. The plan was to continue on to Haast that same night. He was convinced that because his group finished first that his group clearly went higher and was therefore superior to all the others.

"I'm sorry, did we <u>not</u> just climb the same glacier? You just went faster than us."

"Yeah but *we* went higher than all the other groups, our guide said so."

"Um, Edward, maybe he was just saying that, and did you ever think that by ending early you got LESS time up there?"

"No, and I bet you didn't get to go through crevasses and tunnels, like we did."   *Good God are you twelve?* Maybe we were all just overtired. The only person who was not fall-down exhausted was Vicki, (because she hadn't climbed the glacier) who drove us to the hostel in Haast while we comaed.

◉

I woke up far too tired in Haast, and muscles I didn't know I had, hurt. Also, apparently yesterday Marie had fallen down more than I thought… on one leg she had 13 bruises! One looked like a smiley face. At any rate, the place we slept in reminded me of an asylum; wide hall-ways, white walls, small high windows, the couches and chairs in the common room were 1970's brown and orange tweed, and the place was silent. We got out of there as quickly as possible in the morning.

We drove through the Haast Pass, which according to the Lonely Planet Guide, is supposed to be spectacular. I wouldn't call it spectacular… it was nice… the scenery changed to forests of sunny beach trees that could have had elves gambolling amongst the happy bushes and clean smooth tree trunks, until we tumbled into Rohan. Rohan really is the best way to label the Queenstown area; long brown grasses swayed in the breeze over the hills amongst the rocks. Unfortunately, Eomer was nowhere to be found. *Rats.*

Despite the obvious lack of Rohirrim, Puzzling World is one of the coolest places on the planet and begins with a room of holograms that looked as if they were standing in the middle of the room, or changed as you walked by them. Next was a room of famous faces, 3D Einsteins and Mother Teresas moved and watched you as you walked around the room if you closed one eye. It was a palace of optical illusions. Then we found the best room *ever*. It had a messed up angled floor, ceiling, and walls that wouldn't let you stand straight because your brain kept overcompensating and making you fall over! In this room of perpetual drunken walking and belly laughing, there was a pool table with a ball that rolled up, clear pipes with water that fell from a spout and then ran up, and all sorts of confused-gravity devices. At the end, you literally tumbled out of the room like a cartoon character howling like a hyena.

Next came the forced perspective room, where the most brilliant photo of Marie and I was taken. We are in the same room, but I look hobbit sized, and she is a giant. The room was built on angles with the lines and squares on the floor and walls changing in size depending on where they were in the room. The doors were also 'to scale' so to one side Marie was bent over beside a door, and I was barely at the knob of the other only a few meters away. However at a given distance the doors appeared to be the same size. Cool. Before we left we also attempted and succeeded at their 3d Maze, I say succeeded only because I was not in charge here.

Late afternoon we finally arrived into the downtown core of Queenstown and smiled at the cobblestone roads and pointed, sculpted, painted architecture that attempted to give quaintness to all the neon signs, shops, and bars. We stayed at a hotel right near lake Wakatipu, which is backed by The Remarkables, capped and weaved with snow, and fully alive with the sound of screaming. The only downside to Queenstown is that everything was ridiculously expensive. Even the hotel rooms were overpriced and we really couldn't afford a room for four people, unless we went to the dodgy student backpackers at the edge of town. So we lied to the owner and ordered a room for three. We were only staying there for two nights and were fairly sure that if we ninjad our way into the hotel in pairs that no one would be the wiser.

◉

A few weeks before, Edward had talked me into doing the Canyon Swing. Initially I was pretty jazzed about the whole thing, but when it came to paying at the counter the day before, I froze. I was sitting by the window, on the verge of completely backing out, when Edward sat down beside me, and looked into my eyes with complete support:

"Jess, when are you ever going to be in Queenstown again?"

"Never."

"And when will you be here, right now, with *This* opportunity?"

"Probably never."

"And a week ago you wanted to do this remember?! You wanted to do it on our last trip!"

"Yeah..."

"Well what are you waiting for!? Just do it!"

I managed to emit the tiniest of groans.

"Jess, I know you're scared, but it's going to be FUN, and if you don't do it you will regret it for the rest of your life and be like 'Why the hell didn't I do that?!'."

The next morning at 9am, Edward and I climbed onto a rickety bus with a few other people, drove out to the middle of nowhere, with full intention of jumping off a cliff 109 meters high and getting up to speeds of 150kph. We reached the top of the cliff, marched through the spindly naked trees, and I think I lost most of the feeling in my fingers. I could see my breath it was so cold. I was past nervous but volunteered to go third in order to get it over with, but I didn't want to go first in case someone died. However, I quickly second-guessed my decision when I discovered that the harness is held together with nothing more than buckles and Velcro. Velcro is what holds the part that attaches you to the rope above, which keeps you from not dying. *Velcro!??!! You have got to be kidding me!*

"Hey don't touch that, what are you doing?"

"Um, mine's Velcro..."

"Velcro is really strong unless you pull it apart!"

The two guys running this insane operation were great. They made lots of jokes and seemed to understand that we were all terrified but gung-ho.

"You know it IS free if you want to go topless."

I finally got up there, moved to the edge and looked down. *Shit this is high! What the F#@k am I doing?!*

"Edward I don't think I can do this." Everyone who was there waiting for their turn cheered me on, and the guys told me to jump whenever I was ready. I took a short breath.

"Fuck it, okay, here I go".

And then nothing happened. I swear my feet were nailed to the platform. My brain and body just wouldn't jump.

To counter act my body's natural defence mechanism against suicide, they got me to stare at a point on the opposite side of the canyon and only think about that point, I picked a branch, and they counted me down from five.

At zero, I ran and leapt into the air. For a moment it wasn't so bad, I was speeding towards the other side of the chasm and my brain literally thought,

Wow! You're flying!!! You're not going to fall!

And then I stopped, held up my Wile E Coyote exclamation-mark sign, and gravity kicked in.

Clinging to the rope in front of me, I shrieked as the racing winds stole the sound from my throat and plummeted to my inevitable death. Once the freefall was over, my brain returned to me after a quick control-alt-delete and I was dangling over ice blue water surrounded by pale bone rock, I quickly let go of the rope and flung myself backwards laughing and swinging with a feeling of release and joy I had never felt before.

The really dodgy part was coming back up. They cranked your rope back up the cliff face once you stop swinging, which sounds like a lovely time for reflection and looking at the view, but instead you think you are going to die. You cannot only hear, but feel your rope get caught and klunk through the pulleys. *Please don't let the pulleys break my Velcro rope.*

When I reached the platform and was being unhooked I had the biggest grin on my face and would have gone again, if not for the obscene price. Edward went twice, and in crazy positions both times (upside down!), not screaming once, and completely blazé about the whole thing! The only part that irked me was when we were telling the girls about our jump and he declared that his jumps were somehow better than mine.

Afterwards, Edward, Marie, and I went up the Gondola to the top of the hill – aptly called Mt. Bob - and rode the Luge, which is basically a three-wheeled go-cart, while Vicki wandered the city. In the evening, we returned to the hostel for an early night, and as we were watching 'Harry Potter and the Philosopher's Stone' on T.V., our Irish neighbour poked his head into our room, and asked us what we were doing. We all looked up in unison "Watching Harry Potter."

"Oh. Um, so do you guys want to come out for a drink then?"

We lethargically didn't make any attempt at physical movement.

"Uh, maybe after the movie, when are you going?"

"Later on, I'll come and get you when we're going to leave, right?"

He never did come back...

○

The gang appeased me the next day by driving up to Deer Park Heights on our way to Te Anau. I had found a Lord of the Rings Locations Guide book in a bookshop the day before, and realized that a gorgeous Rohan scene was filmed on the way to our next stop. We arrived and discovered that the owners had decided to make you pay 20$ to get in with your car. I figured we could walk up, but Marie was the only one that came with me, and after a bit of a walk and a look at our map, we realised that 5km uphill is actually really far, so we decided to turn back broken, sad, Lord of the Rings fans. To our surprise, Edward and Vicki had been chased by a Bison, and the owner's car, which had been blocking the not-for-public-use entrance, was gone! So we climbed into our car and went around the paying barricade.

The lake the refugees walked around during the Two Towers is a lot smaller than I thought, but I couldn't get a decent picture of the lake reflecting the mountains be-cause a helicopter decided to land right in front of it and wrecked it with its wind. I think it was part of one of those über-geek-really-expensive-LOTR tours. You have got to be dedicated to pay for a private helicopter. We walked around Rohan, gazed appreciatively at the amazing views, and then ran into a Korean prison.

On top of the hill, next to the LOTR lake, is a Korean prison set, from a 1980's Disney movie called "The Rescue"! It's quite broken down now but still has a painting of a staunch Korean leader on the front, and barbed wire and scary fences to keep criminals in... or out... this is just a set after all.

Deer Park Heights is also a Zoo, with sheep, goats, bison, miniature ponies, ostriches, and bison running around. We had a small road blockage from a fuzzy golden-brown Highland-cow that looked like a stuffed toy, and of course, Marie decided that she wanted a *Really* good picture of the ostrich so she rolled down the window and the ostrich came straight for us. Luckily through much shouting and flapping of arms, we got the window up before it could get its head in the car, and managed to magician our way past the Scottish-bovine road guard.

◉

We arrived in Te Anau quite late that night and stayed in a very weird room. First of all when we walked in, there were no duvet covers or sheets because you had to pay $15 for each bunk bed, which by the way didn't have a ladder. We didn't bother paying for sheets, and instead just turned up the space heater. However, Marie touched the temperature gauge and the whole thing shut off and died. We tried to go back to the front desk and get bedcovers but it was too late and the office was dark and locked. I was very thankful for my ugly grey fleece blanket that night. At any rate, there was still a shower, and kitchen to make noodles in. Except the shower and kitchen were in the same room, so if you had a shower, you closed the curtain and flooded the kitchen.

As Vicki and Edward sat down at the wooden obtrusion from the wall I am assuming was meant to be a shelf

-table to study the road, I noticed from my bunk that something was carved into the wall. Our room was outfitted not only with bunk beds and a sink, but also with a floor to ceiling Star of David sunken into the large white painted bricks, and as I curled up on my coat as a pillow and tried to cover myself with my gray fleece blanket, I wondered where I was.

DO IT AFRAID

Chapter 11

A Momentary Lapse of Sanity

The people in the South Island are very nice but... odd. Not only are there no clothes dryers or central heating systems, but also somewhere just southwest of Gore, where we were to meet up with Tara, is a small town whose welcoming sign is covered in crosses and says, "Thank God Jesus is Alive". I am not joking. There is no sign telling you the population, or that police station is to the right and the gardens are to the left; just this.

"Edward, keep driving. Don't stop here." Suddenly I understood the hostel in Te Anau.

◙

After a night spent at Tara's house in Gore watching Shrek 2 at the old movie theatre and eating Lasagne, we arrived in Dunedin quite early the next day. This part of the country looks a lot like the Waikato region in the North Island, with more sheep. Before we went for dinner, we walked up the Steepest Street in the World. According to the Guinness Book of World Records it has a gradient on 1 out of 1.266 – whatever that means.

What can I say about Baldwin St.? Who the crap lives on the top of that hill?! We walked it mostly out of principle, but also out of fear that our car wouldn't make the gradient and would roll backwards into traffic. We ran down it.

We were lucky enough to stay at family friends of Marie's in Dunedin, which meant that we had really good Korean food for dinner. They didn't have central heating either, but at least were fully armed with an arsenal of space heaters and electric carpets (*I mean that literally, their carpets were electric*). Somehow on the way, our car ended up looking like we had driven it through a bog. So we sent Edward out with a hose to clean it up, while we stayed inside the nice warm house and watched Bridget Jones' Diary.

It was here that the extravaganza finally took its toll. When we washed our clothes in the washer, and then misunderstood that there was no dryer, I felt like I was going to cry and yell and throw myself to the floor in a magnificent tantrum. I tried to not be upset, as I was a guest in someone's home, but the lack of clothes dryers was now no longer quaint; it was wrong and potentially blasphemous. I relegated myself to the room I had been given to quietly collect myself. Marie must have felt my ridiculous pain and came in lying down on the bed with me.

"Are you okay?"

"Yeah, I'm just feeling, I dunno, I shouldn't be this upset over wet clothes." I said through sniffs.

"They will dry! They're by the fire now."

"Yeah?"

"Are you feeling homesick?"

"Yeah. I miss home, and Edward's bugging me, and - I'm *tired*."

"It's been a long trip."

"Yeah. It's like we've done so much on this trip we haven't had time to relax at all 'cause we don't want to miss anything. I'm sorry, I'm stupid. We've done so much I'm feeling overwhelmed I guess."

"No, you are not. You just need some sleep, and a hug."

Sometimes the best hugs are from girlfriends.

"Still like me?"

"Yup! Do you still want to eat dinner?"

"Yeah, yeah of course. I just needed to be alone and quiet for a minute you know?"

"Yeah. Hey, I was thinking, off topic, but, for International Night, what do you think of red and black fabric around the room?"

A few minutes later I felt better and was about to come out and visit when I heard Vicki scream "OH SHIT!!!" and Edward laughing hysterically.

"What happened?"

"Vicki just deleted all of her pictures from the trip."

"ALL of them?! How?"

groan "You know that option to format your card? Well it means delete."

Wet clothes and fatigue really don't compare to mistakenly deleting hundreds of photos from your camera.

◉

The next day we went to the Train station, which resembles a castle and has beautiful carved green and white borders on the inside walls, along with stained glass windows, mosaic floors, white archways, high ceilings, and a restaurant. At the restaurant we were served, by a handsome red-haired Scottish lad to blaring Elvis music, a bowl of meat they dared to call lasagne.

Afterwards, we had the obligatory stop at the Cadbury Chocolate Factory, which we had to book the night before because the tours, for obvious reasons, booked up fast. Marie, and I were SO excited we could barely stand it. Meg had said that they give you free chocolate. Lots of free chocolate. We entered into a shiny gold and purple room of chocolate bars glued onto the walls as bricks, and into mountains. It even smelled like chocolate. We were to wait as patiently as possible in this room and the adjacent for the tour to begin.

In the other room there were a series of brightly coloured posters detailing how chocolate is made, and in the very centre was a large wicker basket filled with raw cacao beans for us to taste. NEVER DO THAT. I, like everyone else, popped one into my mouth and crunched down, before making the most revolting downward face while muttering obscenities, and spat it as discreetly as I could into the garbage can which just happened to be placed right beside it. What fool put one of those in his mouth and thought "You know, if I add some sugar and milk to this it's going to be awesome!" ?

The bitter opening for the tour should have been a clue that the whole thing was going to be slightly disappointing. First of all, we only were given 4 mini chocolate bars over the course of the whole tour. Four. Next, most of the machinery wasn't running, so we mostly looked through windows at white machines doing nothing while being told that when they are operational they make a certain kind of chocolate bar. *Yay?* I guess we all had visions of a Charlie and the Chocolate Factory kind of tour. One with funny hats, and edible grass. Maybe a musical number done by small orange people. Still it was fun when we got to sit in old-fashioned purple cars outside, and then watch the 5 STOREY HIGH chocolate waterfall.

After this rather dissatisfying tour, we drove to Larnach Castle, which was rife with ghost stories. It was a big house, built by William Larnach for his wife Eliza. The only room of real note was the boudoir of Constance. Inside among the dim lighting and heavy drapery were mannequins dressed up in her clothes below one hanging from the ceiling like a ghost in a white gown. It was creepy. It felt heavy and … not right. I am not sure if this was the room where the supposed ghost is meant to be, but I wanted to leave that room as quickly as possible.

The view from the top was as usual, stunning, and down below the gardens had been done in an Alice in Wonderland theme, with little hidden stone statues all around. The Cheshire Cat in the tree was slightly creepy. We also found a wishing well, and the throne for the Queen of Hearts, which was fun as we all took various poses on it for the camera.

◙

We left early the next morning for another long driving day to Mt. Cook (the tallest peak in all of New Zealand at 3754m), at Edward's request which meant that we travelled through the Canterbury Plains where gigantic, snow covered mountains spring majestically out of the earth, and towered over a flat brown plain and the ice turquoise waters of Lake Tekapo.

As we neared the famed mountain, the most New Zealandish thing EVER happened. We ran into sheep in the middle of the highway, led by a burly shepherd and his dogs. The sheep were literally blocking traffic. We whooped and squealed with excitement, stopped the car, and took a million pictures, which included inadvertently recreating the cover of our Lonely Planet Guide. The shepherd then shook his stick and yelled obscenities at us for blocking traffic. *I'm sorry, you have 500 sheep on the highway, and WE are blocking traffic?* We apologized but then smirked at the three other cars doing exactly the same thing before moving on to Mt. Cook for a photo op and then continue on to our final stop on our Road Trip Extravaganza.

We arrived at Christchurch in the evening to discover that it has more one-way streets than Wellington, and that is saying a lot. As well, we must have tried seven hundred backpackers, but for some unknown reason, they were all full. All of them. And some places were actually annoyed that we asked to stay there. Four I suppose is too many to house in this city. We ended up staying at "Cokers" backpackers, which was originally built as a swanky hotel over 125 years ago, with Rudyard Kipling of all people staying here.

They opened up the summer wing just for us and gave us a space heater, which we emphatically banned Marie from moving, touching, or breathing on. The décor of Cokers was really neat! All over the brightly coloured hallways were paintings and inspirational messages, and the kitchen was huge and perfect for making a dinner. However, we were too tired to make anything so we went to Denny's for hamburgers, except for Marie who stayed behind in an attempt to make rice. I say attempt because when we got back we found out that she had managed to turn rice, inside a rice maker, into a rock.

◉

July 10th, Marie and I drove to the Antarctic Centre. Where we first willingly subjected ourselves to the cruel elements of the Antarctic's simulated blizzards. We donned our special snow boots and red parkas and then waited with anticipatory anticipation in real snow near a real igloo for the cold bite of blizzard death. First it went kind of dark. Then there was an announcement that it was now minus 40, and to prepare ourselves for the winds. Holy WIND BATMAN!!!! It was frikin freezing! Even for a Canadian! Everyone was all huddled and bundled up and having their curses lost to the wind except for two guys who decided to go in their boxers and bare feet and stand right in front of the wind-chill machine. *Smart.* After the blizzard was over and we all survived, we played on the snow hills and hid in the igloos like little kids until the voice over told us to get out.

There were so many things to see and play with at the Antarctic Centre, fake ice caves, stuffed animals, videos, and snowmobiles, and satellites, and talking holograms! Later on we took our pre-booked ride on the Häaglund, the transport they use in the Antarctic. It started out on a rocky course where the driver showed off all the things the transport could do. We rode up super steep hills, and down very steep hills, and then drove right over crevasses! And when we thought, "Well this is neat, but I'm not *overly* impressed", we felt a clunk and saw we were sinking in a deep pool of water. We glanced at each other with looks of "um... what?" as our driver told us that sometimes in the Arctic the ice breaks, or there isn't any solid ground to drive on, so they made the Häaglund able to go underwater up to a certain depth. The muddy water quickly engulfed our windows and then we noticed that the back door was leaking. Quite a lot actually. But unfortunately we were completely underwater now and had to wait until we hit the bottom before anything could be done. So we edged away from the door, kept our feet off the flooding floor and waited. The Häaglund gently hit the bottom with a few bounces, and when we finally stopped moving, the motor roared to life, and we drove out of our watery grave.

Now that was cool.

After our Antarctic adventure, we met up with Edward and Vicki at the Cathedral. We walked across bridges, and through cobblestone streets that are lined with carved stone buildings and statues of the city, and lit with antique black lampposts that remind me of the 'Lion the Witch and the Wardrobe' while listening to the rumble of the red and yellow streetcars and the distant music of buskers. The Cathedral is at the far end of a large square and is exquisitely detailed with white gothic arches and carved lintels and podiums. You could pay to go to the top of the bell tower, but since I was the only one who wanted to climb the stairs for the view, we didn't go. Marie and I bounced up to the altar and started taking photos of the intricately carved white pulpit and columns, while Vicki freaked out at our obvious irreverent disrespect.

Later, we had a look at the outdoor market in the square. There were many street performers - some were worse than others. There were two guys who could have may or may not juggled... I think... I never actually saw them do anything except say they that were going to do something really cool any minute now...aaaany minute now. There was also a group of young girls, maybe 12 years old, who were dressed up in Victorian cloaks and hats, badly singing pop songs. We ate a ridiculous amount of fish and chips for $4, and then went to the other, cooler, superior markets near the river Avon (on which you can go punting (*how cool is THAT?*)) to meet up with Daniel, Rick, and Ben who happened to be hanging out in Christchurch for their break.

I don't think I have ever seen Edward happier to see three guys before. His face literally lit up like a light bulb and he bounced-ran towards three slightly perplexed boys yelling "HI!!!". I suppose two weeks with only girls in a car must be trying after awhile.

For the evening, Edward and the boys had decided upon some quality beer drinking male bonding time. I'm sure Edward was also pretty desperate for company of the testosterone variety and was happy to not have us women come along. Not that we wanted to come anyway; you couldn't have made us go out that night unless you had offered us an ostentatious amount of money. We were tired and wanted our rest for Hamner Springs the next morning. Edward slunk in to his bunk at an hour that was too late to check the clock.

◙

Vicki decided she didn't want to come to Hamner Springs, so the rest of us packed our bathing suits and climbed into the van for a day in the sun lazing about in resort hot pools, surrounded by mountains. Daniel, Rick, and Ben were behind us in their car by about an hour and a half.

Driving down the road to the springs was lovely, it was a perfectly sunny and gorgeous day and we were all in high spirits. Once we convinced Marie that her navy blue one-piece bathing suit was not too sexy for the hot pools, she sat in the front seat prattling away about nothing in particular, while I daydreamed out the window. I was staring up at a cloud that looked like a giant fox head when suddenly I was violently jolted out of my reverie. I could hear a high screaming as my head bounced off the back of my chair. I wasn't afraid; it was like my mind was watching me from a distance but unaware of what was happening. And then it stopped. The windshield was cracked straight across and I could see Edward's hands were shaking on the steering wheel. Marie was the most coherent of the four.

"Edward, are you okay? What happened?"

"I don't know."

"Jess?"

"Uh huh?"

Edward found his voice. "Jess are you hurt?"

"No."

"Are you sure? 'Cause you were screaming."

"I was?"

"Yeah, you don't know?"

"I heard screaming but I didn't think that was me."

"That was you."

"Oh. Only me?"

Marie piped up in a rather amused voice, as if maybe she didn't understand what had just happened. "One thing I know is I didn't scream. I know because I saw the window crack and I thought 'Oh, we are having a car accident! How interesting.' ha ha ha!"

A gray haired woman worriedly tapped on our window.

"Are you alright?"

"Yeah we're fine."

"Christ, are you sure?"

"Yeah. What happened?"

"What happened? You drove into the other lane and hit two cars, and they hit other cars. I was behind you and saw everything, the police are on their way."

I looked at and Edward and felt a deep pit in my stomach. Edward and Marie got out of the car and slowly looked at the damage, the front passenger side tire was bent under the car and the door was nearly smashed in. I couldn't move. I saw Marie give Edward a long hug as he shook. I found my feet and got out. The woman was talking to them.

"No one was hurt mate, you guys are lucky. That wood cart flew logs everywhere. One smashed through the back window of that lady over there, missed her by nothing."

Why aren't we being yelled at?

The police finally showed up and talked to each of us individually in the back of the police car. The officer was nice to me, but I felt really stupid. I couldn't answer any of his questions, not what happened, not the time, nothing. I wasn't paying attention in the back of the car. He told us that Edward had fallen asleep and swerved into the oncoming traffic. We totalled two cars, including our own, and wrecked another three, not to mention the wood cleanup. Edward was in trouble.

"How long will you be in Christchurch?"

"Today. We were flying back to Auckland today. I'm going back to Canada tomorrow."

"Tomorrow?"

Edward hung his head ready for punishment.

"You know you will have to postpone your trip back for court?"

"Yeah."

There was a long pause as the officer thought out the situation

"You see, in New Zealand, falling asleep at the wheel is considered reckless endangerment. It's a big deal. ... Are you planning on ever returning to New Zealand?"

"No. Probably not."

"Alright then. This is what I'm going to do for you. Instead of staying here for court and possible jail time, I am going to let you go on the stipulation that you can't ever come back."

" I won't."

Did he just get banned from a country?

Lucky for us, Rick, Daniel, and Ben were an hour behind us and picked us up at the petrol-station where the police officer dropped us off and waited with us until the boys came with their little car.

"You sure you're all going to fit in there, mate?"

Ben answered as Rick and Daniel made themselves scarce in the petrol-shop.

"Oh yeah, heaps of room, no worries." But none of us got into the car until that policeman was well out of sight. We put Edward into the trunk, the rest of us squashed ourselves into the car, and the girls ate Edward's chocolate. 6 people in a 5-person car.

For dinner Edward and Marie made Spaghetti. It was actually really good, but I wasn't in the mood for eating really. Called Mum at 3am her time to tell her about the accident, and texted Louise. Then my fingers texted Noah.

We had really good friends. Our flight back to Auckland was at 9am the next morning, and because we no longer had a car, Rick got up, and drove us to the airport.

I even got to see the sunrise from the airplane. It was stunning, of course not on my side, but beautiful reds and pinks bled through the windows as we flew back to reality.

One thing I noticed on Air New Zealand is that in the emergency foldout there is a section on what is not allowed on airplanes, like cell phones. One of the banned items was a Furby... *How does that affect airline equipment?*

Expanding Paradigms.

Back from holiday and now in desperate need of a vacation from the vacation, amongst new classes and a new and very evil German teacher, International Night was starting to come together. On top of all the preparations, Jazmin decided she really wanted a superb opening number for both after dessert, and for the start of the show. I put her in charge of the opening number and washed my hands of it. Her vision for post-dessert was the song "Desert Rose" by Sting in a dreamlike dramatic dance sequence. Initially I had no idea what she meant at all especially since she couldn't really show me, but she was so inspired that I had to go along with it. Now I'm a decent dancer, but she blows me out of the water, and I certainly have never choreographed anything before; this was completely out of my league. She had the image of three couples in ball gowns and top hats amid swirling smoke. She dragged Suvik over to my room one day, and talked him into being our first guy. I had never met him before and he seemed shy, but willing to play along. He was from Sri Lanka and his arms looked like he lifted heavy things in his spare time. We later moved into the music room and I asked Jackie to join our dance, which she did with gusto and about 500 ideas.

Desert Rose is exactly 4 minutes and 49 seconds long.

You have no idea how excruciatingly long that can be until you have to come up with something brilliant to do for 4 minutes and 49 seconds, with no previous choreography experience.

Once we had the beginning sort of figured out, we realised that we needed the rest of the guys now. All of the really good dancers were the Indian boys, but they were knee-deep in choreographing their own Bollywood number with their girls, '... and Noah couldn't do it because he was too short, which sucked because he would have been perfect for the role. Jazmin and I had envisioned an Alpha Male dancer... which is hard to find in a university hostel. And then, one night, walking by the games room, I spotted Daniel and Rick playing pool. Perfect height, perfect build, decently looking, and I had seen them holding rhythm amongst all their air-guitaring at dance clubs; the only problem is talking two rugby-playing-beer-drinking-male-engineers to be in a dance with music by Sting.

"Hey guys, would you be interested in being in a dance for International Night? We need two more guys..."

"Um... no, we don't dance" says Daniel.

(*Jess gives doe eyes*) "But we need two strong guys who can hold a basic rhythm and lift us and stuff, we can show you, it won't be hard, it'll be fun,..."

"OH! Oh, we can be lifters!" says Daniel now completely changing his mind.

Although I think they nearly backed out once they saw the 20 seconds of dance we had come up with. Their faces went slack the first time they saw Suvik dancing with Jazmin. To be honest, we didn't know what we were doing, and it could have looked like crap, but it was coming along, and at least the basic feel and genre should have come through.

The first hurdle was acting on the guys part, we knew

what we wanted them to do, but being girls, and not directors, we couldn't "speak guy" to communicate it across to them.

"Like you need to be circling like a vulture, like a vampire, threatening but adoring at the same time, um... assertive?"

I broke down and got Noah. For all his idiosyncrasies he was the one person I knew who could pull it off without thinking.

"Guys, you need to look at them like: Oh *yeah* I'm going to F&@X her tonight".

I felt a wave of embarrassment as Noah circled me for his example using progressively perverse colourful language to get his point across. But then, suddenly, the mist parted and all the guys were on the edge of their seats nodding their heads like school children. Men.

◉

Another thing I had yet to do was get ridiculously drunk. And then magically, as if the Gods themselves had ordained it, IH Orientation week (Second Semester) finished off with a Pub Crawl. Do I remember the pub-crawl? Most of it. I decided to join because I had chickened out on the last one, had never been on a pub-crawl, and Phil, Tom, Jenn, Daniel, and Kate (a new redheaded artist pal with a penchant for using the word "fuck" as an all-purpose adjective from England) were going. If ever a time to go on a pub-crawl, this would be it. Back in Ontario I had never even really had a drink let alone go to a nightclub with a bunch of drunken people past midnight. I was told by my mother ever since I was a little girl what ladies do and don't do, and ladies don't get drunk on a pub-crawl or stay out late, that's the kind of situation that can only lead to bad.

We bumbled onto the red double-decker bus with a

few people from the Railway Campus residence, and were instructed by our student council president that we were not allowed to start drinking until we left the alcohol ban zone. *You can drink on a bus?* I sat beside Kate who had brought some coolers with her to share with me.

"Darling, tonight we are going to get you completely shattered.

Shattered? I don't want to drink so much that I break!" Laughing.

"Ah, we'll take care of you luv, won't we Tommy!?"

"Yes!" Tom rubbed his ostentatiously silver shirt "And maybe, you'll even like it."

Oh boy here we go.

The announcement of the alcohol-banned zone was received with loud cheers and the cracking open of bottles and cans. We went from bar to bar, dancing, and taking tequila shots, remembering less and less.

It was here that I finally learned how to grind on the dance floor. At probably the second club, Tom grabbed my hand and dragged me up to the floor.

"Come here babe we are gonna dance so they stare!"

"What? No! I dunno how to dance like that."

He grinned and grabbed my hips, pulling himself intimately close to me and started dancing. It took all of 20 seconds for me to get the movement, throw my arms around his neck and start to have some fun with it. I was spun, dipped and ground, and it was fun. Really really fun. Kate catcalled at the side, and when the song was over she strutted in and took the next dance.

When we arrived at the third club I realised I had too much. Far far too much. I had to get out of the bus, and I really don't remember how I got down the stairs, but I do remember Phil's arm around my waist in support on the road, and walking me to the door and through the bouncer. He sat me down and asked how I was feeling.

"Really dizzy."

Jenn had come over to see what was up.

"Jess is drunk isn't she!? Yes!"

"Quite possibly. I'm just really dizzy."

"Water. Sit. Stay."

Jenn brought me a very large glass of water and lorded over me until I drank the whole thing, while Phil ensured that I wasn't going anywhere, by keeping a hand on my shoulder. Phil then got up to get me another glass of water, while Jenn bounced off to dancing and merriment. In my 4min alone, Daniel sat down beside me and asked how I was doing.

"Fine. Dizzy. Just dizzy. I'm supposed to drink water, and Jenn said I wasn't allowed to dance anymore."

"Yup, yup, makes sense. My child, I think you have had too much."

Phil returned with the glass of water and the boys exchanged eyes. Phil handed me the glass and left. Jenn returned, brought me another glass of water once I had finished my second, and then instructed Daniel, as he was clearly now my keeper, to not let me get up from that chair. At all. Ever. Unless I was going to be sick. I didn't understand why she was so adamant on these rules of drinking, especially when I started to feel better, and saw Tom dancing away with Kate not too far from me.

"I think I'm going to go and have a dance, I'm feeling lots better."

Daniel grabbed my wrist and firmly held it down on the arm of the chair.

"No your not."

"Yes I am!"

"No."

I was confused. I tried moving my arm, but he was much stronger than me, and sat calmly in his chair looking resolute in his decision. The foot had gone down.

"Lemme go?"

"No."

Jenn bounced back and I winged that Daniel wasn't letting me go. Jenn threw her head back and laughed.

"Good! He's doing his job!"

Daniel nodded in approval, and I was forced to wait out this leg of the pub-crawl attached to a chair.

For the last two clubs I elected to not have any more drinks, and settled for socialising, and occasionally skank -dancing with Tom as he scanned the room for potential boyfriends (for him not me). I must say that this was an experience that I am glad I had, but would not necessarily want to repeat. I don't think I need to see a line of boys peeing on a fence again.

The Dance That Could Possibly May or May Not Be of Love.

As Desert Rose progressed we discovered that not only was Noah a good choreographer, but so was Jackie, me, and our flamboyant friend Tom, whom we started to call "director". He had a talent for the romantically dramatic that worked for us; unfortunately he took to writing down on what beat we were off, so we kept on being told things like

"You were off on the 3rd beat on the 9th section". *What does that even mean?* However, Jackie was the only one with real live choreography experience, so she and I basically ran the show. As well, once we moved rehearsal to the squash courts, Noah disappeared into the abyss of IH, never to be heard of again. Nevertheless, all of us were really quite proud of what we had accomplished and were enjoying the whole creative process.

Jackie and Rick had been placed together by Jazmin, as had Daniel and I, and it seemed that Jackie and Rick took a fancy to each other. Actually it was rather cute, and soon they were an official couple. As the weeks progressed it looked like Daniel also had a twinkle in his eye whenever we danced, and took the time to hang out with me more. Jackie was convinced that he liked me, but I really thought that since it was obvious he liked Abby, that the twinkle was just from acting like he was meant to in the dance. It took him ages to look like that, and besides Abby was sporty and liked to drink, and Daniel and I didn't really have that much in common. And yet Jackie was adamant, and there was an awkward energy between us. She was convinced that if he was going to make a move it would be at the Ball. So I crossed my fingers, got my mom to send me a different formal dress, because the one I was using for Desert Rose had already been seen, and waited.

The night before the Ball, a bunch of us girls took over the common room to do our nails and I asked Louise do my hair in pin-curls so I would look amazing the next night. We had music playing and chocolate for everyone. A few boys opened the door to come in, but slowly backed out once they saw the sea of estrogen and pyjamas.

The next day I did my makeup, put on my dress, fixed my curls, and went to Jackie's room for last minute silliness. Kate had arrived there too, and so the three of us chatted away until Jackie remembered that she had bought some Biltong. This is South African dried meat that comes in chunks, and is wonderfully seasoned. She cut it in thirds and the three princesses, in their finery, sat on a sunken bed gnawing and growling like dogs at dried meat. Suvik knocked-opened the door to see how we were getting along, and then froze when he saw us. "What the HELL." I don't know what his problem was, I think we were very classy.

It was while we were convening in the games room for pre-ball photos and drinks before the bus arrived that I saw Daniel and Rick arrive for the festivities. Rick was dressed as Slash from Guns 'n Roses, and looked ridiculous. Daniel looked worse. He was sporting the ugliest brown and green tartan wool jacket ever, with a gold tie, and a shirt with blue, brown, and yellow squares and circles. It was almost embarrassing. Jackie, being Jackie, thought Rick looked brilliant and ran over for hugs and pictures, while I tried my best to not look horrified. Marie looked amazingly beautiful, and "the boys" looked very 007.

In the ballroom, I walked with Jackie over to a table in the far corner where Daniel and Rick were seated, and sat down. The first words out of Rick's mouth were "That's Abby's spot."

"What?" I tried to laugh.

"Abby is sitting there."

I turned to Daniel who just sat there looking uncomfortable, so I shrugged my shoulders and sat down beside him anyway.

They may be dressed like idiots but I'm not getting ousted from the table like the un-popular kid like before. Abby returned to the table in a simple blue dress, looked at me, and sat at another seat not too far away. Dinner came and went, and then the waltz started. Daniel and I had been taking ballroom lessons together at O'Rorke residence for the ball and he had promised me a waltz. Jackie and Rick got up and left for the dance floor. I turned to Daniel.

"So are we gonna go?"

"Uh, it seems kinda crowded."

"Yeah,"

"Maybe wait until the next waltz, less people will be there."

"Oh." I said trying to mask my disappointment as I watched the hundred other couples swirl together. "Okay. If that's what you want to do." There never was another waltz.

The rest of the night I tried to dance, chat and be silly and have fun, but mostly all I could think of was that Daniel was desperately trying to avoid me, and blatantly flirting with Abby. I could have died and he wouldn't have noticed. I felt SO stupid for believing Jackie, for hoping that he liked me. I knew he never did but I thought there was a possibility so I went and made expectations all on my stupid own and now felt dejected. I tried to hang out with my friends, and had some fun, but there was a drop in my heart. It would have been better if I had gone with the expectation of being alone. It wasn't like I was unaccustomed to going to a ball stag. Even for my high school prom I went without a date, which I actually really wanted, because I was afraid it would make a friend of mine upset with me.

Jackie was sorry for my 'misfortune' and Desert Rose rehearsals continued as they did before, except that Daniel kinda stopped looking at me. The sparkle had left his eye and he didn't help me off the floor anymore at the end of the song. He'd just get up, and walk away. He spoke sharper to me now like he was annoyed with having to even be around me, and at the end of rehearsal he couldn't get out of that room fast enough. He was still going with us on our last vacation trip, and Jackie thought that maybe something could happen there, but I was unconvinced. She was still certain that he liked me, Abby or not, but it was pretty obvious which one he wanted. *I am such a stupid girl.*

◉

International Night had also finally hit a giant snag. Marie, the sweet girl that she is, was not holding up her end and I was about ready to have her killed. I had asked her for drawings of the backdrop weeks before. Not only had she not done that, she hadn't a clue what to do, and her fabric idea had become my responsibility because she apparently couldn't go to fabric stores because she didn't know "what I wanted". It even took both Louise and I to explain to her how to measure the perimeter of a room. Secretly, I started talking to Kate. Kate was also an art student, and even though she was a nut, she spoke and acted like she meant it.

"Kate, I'm starting to freak about Marie. She's just not doing anything! I mean if she brought be drawings and measurements or something to show she is at least working on it, I'd be okay, but this is getting stupid!"

"What is she supposed to do?"

"Besides the red and black fabric fiasco? The backdrop. That's what I'm worried about. Kate, I know this feels like backstabbing, but could you maybe do it instead of her?"

"Like how?"

"Well, it's supposed to be in 3 panels to give the groups as much flexibility in coming on stage as they need, but I don't know what should be on them. And neither does she.

I brought out a few sketches I had done on my own.

"Like I was thinking maybe something that shows different ecology around the world? Like keeping it international but still kinda pretty?"

Kate took one look at my picture and glanced at me with a 'no.'

"What not a good idea?"

"Too busy. Alright, hang on." She took out some pencil crayons. "What about this?"

She swiftly drew three panels covered in blue and silver swirls.

"Wow. That's good."

"Yeah, I thought so, and it'll look great with your Desert Rose bit."

"Ooooh. Yeah it will! Okay. So, you'll help?"

"Of course love. But how will you break it to Marie? I don't want to start anything."

"Yeah... Well.. I was thinking that we don't break it to her. Like, maybe if you told her that you have this great idea for the backdrop and you really want to help, that she would be fine with a gung-ho helper. So she thinks you are 'helping', but you are really 'doing'. That way her feelings won't get hurt but the backdrop will still get done."

God I feel guilty about this. Is this being mean or a leader? How can I just trust her if she hasn't shown me any reason to?

Chapter 14

A Legitimate Vacation

The exciting thing about this trip is that we had no plans! This fine sunny morning, Jackie, Louise, Kate, and I fell out of bed, had some form of breakfast, and met up at the Sky Train station for the five-dollar bus ride down to Tauranga with our non-IH friend Sam (who I met rather unceremoniously in our Greek Tyranny class as we tried to stay awake through a nonsensical 'points' game whereby we got points for doing good things, high marks, being silly or cheeky or... for no reason at all. As well as trying to not lose our minds every time we read the word 'Ptolemy' in our study notes.) It was an excruciatingly long bus ride; filled with sitting at the very back of the bus, blue skies, sheep, biltong, dried mango, black-balls, and then a heart-attack.

"Uh, Louise, what did you just call this candy?"

"Nigger-balls. What? That's what they're called."

I tried to have some composure.

"I thought they were black-licorise-balls...because they are black licorise...and they are balls..."

"Well yeah, but we call them nigger-balls in South Africa."

"Ohmygod. Um. Stop calling them that. Someone's gonna hear you!"

"Sam, we call them nigger-balls in South Africa aye?"

"Yup, yup some do! But I don't think Jess is ever gonna! She's from Canada remember? They wouldn't say that word."

"But Jess you know I didn't mean it in a bad way. You know I'm not racist."

"In North America, anyway is a bad way. You don't say that. Ever."

"Alright, relax."

Jackie was beyond giddy with the thought of going home and seeing her family, and was tittering with excitement and bounce, once we drove back into cell phone territory. By the time we reached Tauranga it was four hours later and my bum was sore. Rick was meant to pick us up at the stop, but Rick being Rick, was late. He eventually drove up in a 70's ghetto gray van with seat belts that only sort of worked and we all piled in for, yes, another... long...drive to Whakatane and Jackie's house.

Considering we were all still very wide awake from sitting and doing nothing all day we decided to head on up to the lookout point – in the dark. In the middle of winter. Guess what? It was dark and cold. We saw... dark, not even stars because the moon was out, and hoped the dreaded Taniwha wouldn't leap out of the ocean and kills us all. I think the point was to see the moon reflecting over the sea, but by the time we got there the moon had moved out of the cool reflection zone. So we assumed it was nice during the day, went back, and all climbed into our borrowed sleeping bags on the floor of the backroom while Jackie and Rick fought for the good mattress. It wasn't that they both wanted it; it was that they both were trying to give it to the other but were both far too stubborn to accept it. I am surprised that Jackie held out for so long, Rick is twice her size and can be found chopping wood at home. I solved the problem in a moment of tired frustration, when the two of them half-leap-rolled on top of me at the climax of this fight, by suggesting that they both sleep on the comfy mattress since it was so big.

◉

I woke up the next morning to the sun gently warming my blue sleeping bag, and to the not too distant sound of sheep. *Sheep? YES! That's Brilliant!* There are sheep right across from Jackie's house and you can hear them! It's great! I could have stayed on her balcony all day looking at the emerald hills and listening to soft bleating under the blue sky. But we had a plan to go Ohope to pick up Daniel and then drive to Taupo to pick up Phil and Jonny, to get to Mt. Ruapehu to play in the snow. Which didn't happen because of our problem with the concept of "early"... We woke up, doddled around, made eggs and toast for breakfast and then lazed our way over to Daniel's house by the crack of eleven. We of course looked like the eager beavers because Daniel was still sleeping. Jackie pounded on the door until a frazzled Daniel appeared and greeted us with "Oh shit!" before ducking back into the dark house

Jackie retorted "Nice to see you too matey".

The rest of us walked down to Ohope beach and waited for him to...do...whatever... guys...do...to get ready. It took like an hour, although he maintains that it was only 20 minutes. Not that that was a problem, we quite happily lazed and played on the beach until his arrival. We drew in the sand, Rick made a very cool sandcastle with mud drips, Kate chased Louise around with mud, and Jackie wrote a poem of epic proportions about the beauty of the beach, until Rick ever so gallantly usurped the position of court poet by writing the following: "Every time I see this place, I think Woah." Now that's poetry. Daniel finally showed up, and after the boys threw very large rocks into the sea, we piled into the car and headed south.

As I approached Taupo for now the second time I could see the three snow-covered mountains in the blue distance, Tongariro, Ruapehu, and Ngarehoe. We finally received a text from Phil as we neared the town with the message that he is busy until at least 6 o'clock. Since we still had an entire afternoon to kill we stopped at Huka Falls, which happened to have roosters in the parking lot, which the boys tried to catch. Huka Falls is an absolutely dynamic waterfall that storms down the canyon. We walked to the top lookout and wandered back down with the idea of driving to Lake Taupo and feeding the ducks.

Unfortunately, I hadn't eaten since early that morning at Jackie's house and I was now starving to the point to fainting on the spot. I very politely demanded that we stop somewhere to get meat-pie, which was easy because we had to stop at the supermarket anyway to get bread for Jackie's ducks and chocolate for Phil's mum who was putting us up for the night and now feeding a grand total of eight hungry university students. And so we sat by the lake, eating pie and feeding the ducks. Actually I had never fed ducks from my hand before and I was a little nervous that they might miss the bread and bite off my finger, until Daniel laughed at me and held my hand out with some bread in it for the ducks to feast upon. Very exciting for the city girl. The rest of the day we spent playing in the hot pools, and tossing a beach ball around that eventually turned into a game of monkey in the middle.

Finally we made it to Phil's house where his mum made us a brilliant lasagne for supper, and his step dad showed us card tricks. We also found the best game known to mankind. It is called "Bop It" and is an electronic handheld game where you follow instructions to music – bop it, flick it, spin it, twist it, or pull it. Sounds simple enough but it's not, and when you mess up it insults you "Dude!", "Try again, only Better!". The boys got quite addicted to it and the entire night you could find either Jonny or Rick playing the game while bopping their heads and shoulders to the music.

Later on the boys went out to rent a movie and the girls were introduced to a stick. Now don't get all sexy on me, this was a stick the length of a broom handle (oh stop it.) and Phil's step-dad taught us this twisted, possibly useful for karma sutra, way of getting the stick from behind one's back to in front of you while stepping over it and not letting go of the stick. Why he knew how to do this I will never know. When the boys came back we proudly showed off our new talent to blankly baffled faces. Jonny tried and succeeded, as did Phil. Rick gave it a couple of good goes but failed, and Daniel, well, he tried once and failed miserably, never to speak of the stick again.

Now the boys had thought that watching 'The Ring' would be a fun end to the day, even though they had promised us a cheesy action movie. I protested with threats of sleepwalking and temporary insanity, but they put it on none the less. Rick tried to sneak in the Bop It toy but it was quickly removed from him. I hate that movie. I hated it the first time I saw it and I hated it the second time I saw it, except this time I had a vague idea of when I should close my eyes. I don't like being frightened on that level. This is not a jump-from-a-ghost movie. This is a pee-your-pants and throw-out-your-TV movie. I watched it reluctantly for the second time because really, what else was I supposed to do? Sit in the other room by myself and listen to it? I am surprised that Daniel's arm wasn't permanently damaged with my fingernail marks. When the movie was over, of course, someone's cell phone had to go off and in one terrified leap I managed to hop the entire length of the couch to my great protector who laughed at me. That night we all crammed into one room except for Rick, Phil, and Jonny who kept calling our cell phones and rasping "seven days".

"Jonny, I know its you. I have call display."

".........seven days." click.

Rick seemed to like to stand just outside our door, wait for us to drift into sleep before hitting the Bop It so the music and "And bop it!" would start.

◉

For once we all actually woke up at a decent hour, made tea, and then drove to lake Taupo for brunch. We sat on a picnic table right by the lake in front of a wonderful sign with a little stick-man falling upside down, beside a crumbling rock cliff. Of course, us girls needed to have our photo taken from behind the sign. It was asking for it. The lake was crystal clear and you could see to the bottom for ages, if you weren't marvelling at the sun bursting clouds that had sprouted from the snow-covered mountains in the distance. As we stopped to get some petrol I had the unstoppable urge to sit on the roof of Rick's van, and so I did, with the help of Daniel to get up there. When Rick returned from the cashier he found me perched on top, quite happy, and eating a biscuit. He looked at me with an amused but shocked expression and said "Hyperactive child!" as he easily lifted me down as if I was all of about six years old.

The road to Ruapehu was one I had only driven in the fog before, but when the sun comes out in all its glory, the "Great Desert Road" is fantastic. The reddish brown grass melts in with green thick-leaved plants that are dotted along the plain. Jutting out of the ground are the mountains; most dramatically is the conical Ngarahoe, a.k.a. Mt. Doom. Although it looks substantially less terrifying without the giant fiery red eye atop, covered in a thick blanket of glittering snow. No Orcs either. Rather a disappointment I would say, although it still looks a whole lot like Mt. Doom, so we renamed it as such, but Daniel protested the new name and said that we ought to call it just Doom.

The road was long and winding, and what better way to pass the time on a long car ride than to sing the entire way! I think we sang every single song we ever knew, and the boys just shook their heads, until they overpowered a 'Little Mermaid' Disney song with Led Zeppelin, Kate kept trying to get us to sing jazz, but no-one knew any, so she ended up singing off key by herself while playing wistfully with the string of nuts she stole off of George.

We arrived at Mt. Ruapehu with much excitement and bounce, and then learned something really weird: Sam had up to this point, never seen the snow. Ever. Who would have thought? We also learned that while Louise is small, she fights like a boy, and she bites. Phil started it by trying to push her into the snow, a little too hard. She responded by pushing back. They struggled until he got her in a sort of a chokehold and Louise realised that she couldn't get out of Phil's much stronger arms; then she bit his finger. The rest of the afternoon involved a giant snowball fight, sledding down hills on black garbage bags, and eating lots of candy for sustenance. But mostly covert snowball fights. I was a sneaky bugger and got Sam on my team, she made the balls, and I tossed them. At one point Daniel took at least five snowballs to the head before he realised that it was indeed the little girl sitting innocently on the rock that was to blame. Phil and Jonny were the covert S.W.A.T. team, and Rick and Daniel ended up having a wrestling match in the snow. At one point Jackie and I found the perfect spot for making snow angels to the sound of Louise squealing with childish glee every time she flew down the hill on her garbage bag. It was a good day of fun. The view from the mountain was spectacular, as seems to be the norm in New Zealand; and I bet that the view from the much higher up ski fields would have been even better. Much later on in the day, very wet and sleepy, we headed back to Phil's house for a bowl of pumpkin soup before we continued on to Jackie's house for the night.

◎

September 2nd, was like the days surrounding it, pouring rain. We watched movies, and played the Murder Game until it started to clear up and Jackie's dad offered to take us out on their boat, the Amante. Amante means "mistress" and was so named because Jackie's mum believes that her husband spends more time with the boat than with her. Under deep blue clouds, we pulled out of the wooden dock and headed for the open sea. Passing the woman on the rock, Wairaka, on the way.

Legend tells us that Wairaka's tribe arrived at Whakatane's shores, and as is customary, they left the women in the canoe to go and explore the land. Unfortunately, the boat started drifting off and by the ancient rules of Maori custom, women were not allowed to paddle the boats, but the men were too far away to see them and they were drifting out to sea and certain death. One woman, Wairaka threw the rules out the window, took up an oar, said "Let me act like a man", directed the women to do the same, and steered them back to the sandy beach and safety.

Passing the Maori heroine we entered into the region of the bar. The bar is where the calm bay and the wild Sea meet. It is very choppy and dangerous and I thought that I was going to fall out of the boat. We were smashed and tossed about in the rough waters, salty spray from the ocean in our faces, under a darkening grey sky. Phil very kindly and firmly held onto me so I would not be snatched by the Sea. We couldn't stay out all that long as the clouds got darker and closer by the minute and it became too dangerous to stay out on the water any longer.

That evening we invited Daniel over for a barbeque. He, Phil, and Jonny barbequed, while the girls made salad and I attempted cocktails.

"Jackie, I followed the recipe, but I don't think the drinks are supposed to be bright toxic green."

"Oooh! Neat! Let me try some!" she takes a gulp and laughs, "Jess, this is bloody fantastic! Don't quite know what it is, but it's great! Hey Dad, look at this!"

"Um, that's a ...festive colour you girls have made there."

"Do you want to try some?"

"No."

Of course the men soon started to complain that they were cooking without beer, so we sent Jackie on a beer-mission. I suppose that it's impossible to enjoy raw meat, fire, and grunting, without beer. Tragic really. The boys were brilliant to watch as they all hovered over the flames, Daniel with the fork and flipper, Jonny with the flashlight, and Phil as the bouncer. Every so often one of us girls would venture out onto the balcony to see how they were faring and the Parting-Of-The-Boys would begin, stepping aside and then waiting for an approving word so they could nod and smile and then flip a piece of meat, as if to stress their great barbequing skills, before taking another sip of their beer.

Phil, on the other hand, became very territorial over the balcony and at one point I found myself being lifted up and carried back into the house where "I was meant to be." *Sorry, what?* With that, all the girls went outside. Don't tell me where I am "meant to be", - I will BE, wherever I WANT to BE. The meat was amazing. Louise needed to cook the borovorse (an African sausage) herself, as she didn't trust the culinary skills of the boys. We all became very tiddly on cocktails and beer, including Jackie's mom who really, really liked my neon-green toxic -waste concoction. She liked it a little too much in fact, turning at one point, much to our hilarity, to Jackie and saying with a very serious expression: "Is my face numb?"

We ended the evening with watching movies in the back room until late. And then a funny thing happened during the second movie. Daniel changed his spot on the floor to on the pullout bed beside me, and held my hand, casually playing with my fingers. Up until then I thought that he was interested in Abby. What had changed his mind tonight I just don't know, but I was happy about it. Happy and hoping that he kept his mind changed. Once he left I went up to the washroom to get myself ready for bed and found Jackie already washing her face. I swiftly entered and closed the door.

"Guess what."

Her eyes widened with anticipation "what?"

"Remember how Daniel changed places from the floor onto the bed beside me?

"Yeah I noticed that." She was grinning.

"He held my hand."

"I KNEW it! I knew he liked you and not that sporty little thing! Ha! Oh Jess I am SO happy for you!" She squealed and I noticed I was giggling.

"I know, who knew! He just changed his mind I guess. I really thought he was dating Abby."

"She never had anything on you. Oh this is SO great!"

◙

Kate, Sam, and Rick had to leave for Auckland a little early. Once they had left Jackie and I packed a picnic of leftover barbeque meats and bread, called up Daniel, and headed out to Otawai Bay for lunch. We drove down to the beach and then climbed up through the tall, forested inlet to the Bay. When we reached the very top I climbed over the railing and peered through a break in the trees to the bay below and our destination. Deep green hills surrounded the sparkling turquoise waters, which softly lapped the sandy beach and reflected off of the rocks that melted out into the sea. The walk was long and mostly up, except for when we went down, but eventually we reached the beach, laid out our towels under the shelter of a great Pohutukawa tree, and opened our lunch bucket.

The sand, as I discovered, was not the usual grainy stuff, but tiny polished pieces of shell. In fact the whole beach was littered with big shells and little shells, of all shape and colour, and on one shell-searching expedition I was fortunate enough to find one half of an unbroken Paua shell. Paua is very common in New Zealand jewellery and art but is near impossible to find anywhere but the retail stores and street vendors. Its pearly and rainbow coloured interior makes it quite the hot commodity, and I found one. It's mine! It came to ME!

We spent most of the day looking for seashells, playing Frisbee, climbing trees, and just generally enjoying ourselves by doing very silly things like sticking a finger into a sea anemone just to watch it think we were food. That has to be cruel on some level, but it's so much fun to feel it sucking on your fingertip. I made a sand-pyramid complex, and then began helping Daniel with his stick-shrine. It's always funny to watch the differences between boys and girls with things like this. I took the time to make a little detailed hut and decorated pathway to the main stick shrine area, while Daniel brought over bigger and bigger sticks and shoved them in the ground. I of course knocked over the bigger ones when I could. Louise too came over and built a wall separating his temple from hers and declared her people to be believers of

Louism, and that they wanted nothing to do with the Danites. *The Danites?*

Our initial plan, actually all break, was to have a big bon-fire on Ohope beach, like we had done all those months ago, but apparently the one police officer in all of Ohope had decided to crack down on bonfires, I am convinced, just to ruin our fun. We thought of having it at Otawai, but it was too close to houses, houses that had people inside them who might call the police when they saw fire on the beach. But we decided anyway to see if we could find a camping ground or a barbeque pit anywhere in the area that evening.

We gave up on fire and instead set out for Ohope beach to watch the sunrise. The sky was twinkling and brushed across with the Milky Way. As Daniel and I sat on a hill watching the heavens, we heard Louise and Jackie whooping and laughing in the darkness. Out of curiosity, we sauntered over to see what all the fuss was about. We had stopped on a beach with phosphorescent algae. It was everywhere. You could scoop up the sand and in your hand would be three or four little stars. If you stomped your foot the little lights would appear beneath and all round your feet. And if you threw some sand into the water the little fallen stars would shimmer and hang in the waves. We spent at least an hour tossing sand into the Sea and wiping our hands over the ground to make a glowing trail with much enjoyment and giggles. We would have stayed longer but it was getting very very cold.

We drove back to Daniel's house, parked the car, got some blankets, and then walked down to the beach that we knew so well. I found myself cuddled up with Daniel in blankets on the beach watching the sky, which had gracefully decided to give us a magnificent show of shooting stars. You know for each shooting star, you get a wish if you are the first to see it. Daniel never saw one first. In the darkness you would see a trail of light, and then hear Louise, Jackie, or myself say "Oh! There's one!" and then Daniel go "Dammit!"

We were lucky enough to watch the moon rise too. From the sea rose a blood red disk that illuminated the clouds from behind and reflected onto the water. Once the moon was up, we noticed that this beach too had glowing algae, the sea sparkled merrily, and the soft rolling waves glowed as they approached the shore and started to foam.

Then girls and I decided that we needed chocolate. Except we never bothered to take the chocolate out of the car in the first place. Daniel got up, went to the car and brought it back for us. Jackie promptly dropped a rather large piece into the sand, but figured that the five-minute rule applied so she brushed it off, gave it a shake, and popped it into her mouth. Afterwards we only heard a sandy crunch and the sounds of disgust.

I have never had such a romantic night in my life. I am cuddled up under the a wash of white that softly blended its way into the star-filled crimson clouds, watching the shimmering waves lap the twinkling shore, and eating the most decadent chocolate ever.

While we were counting the shooting stars, out of the corner of my eye I saw movement. I turned my head towards the moving light and saw a star, a very bright star starting to pendulum from its original place. "Guys, is that star moving?" They all sat up and looked to the right, "What the HELL?!" I was not hallucinating, or if I was, then the other three were as well. Soon after it began changing colours from its original white, to a deep blue, to red, to green, to orange, and then back again to white. It zipped and dipped and looped and swirled about the sky, not all over the starry dome, but in one big corner. It did this for hours. We actually eventually got bored of it and went back to watching the shooting stars and the waves. I suppose my defence for our blaséness over the phenomenon was that it posed us no danger, never came any closer, and just flew around without any pattern. Every once in awhile it would drift back to its original place and sit there like a normal star, before getting bored and go gambolling about the sky again. We joked about being the representatives for earth (there goes the planet), and then continued on waiting for the sun to rise.

Not an hour later, we heard footsteps behind us in the grass and the crack of a twig. Considering it was around three in the morning, and there were no voices, Daniel took the flashlight and shone it up onto grass to see who was there and if we ought to leave or not. He never saw anyone. Nothing at all, and considering that it is a flat plain with grasses that leads to the road, it would be difficult for a person to hide, even in the tall ones. We sat back down and started to settle, and then we heard the rustling of grass and the snap of a twig again. And so we looked again, and saw nothing. There are no squirrels or any kind of large wild animal here, and dogs just aren't that stealthy. And it didn't sound like an animal, it sounded like something bigger that was sneaking. I looked over my shoulder and the changing-colour-flying-all-over-the-place-star was in full swing. Right. We decided to listen to our instincts, forgo the sunrise and go home. There was clearly someone in the tall grasses, very close to us, you could sense it, but even with our flood-lamp of a flashlight none of us could see where. So we walked to the car and drove back to Jackie's house to catch some sleep before my bus ride back to Auckland with Louise in the morning.

Rehearsal

When we got back to IH, Jazmin decided that even though it was her idea in the first place, she couldn't be in Desert Rose anymore because of schoolwork and the Indian dance. Immediately, Suvik thought the new Chilean girl Bachata would be a good replacement. I didn't think so, mostly because I didn't like her. When I first met her in the dining hall and asked for her name she replied "Bachata". The table went silent. So I smiled and said "Bachata? Like... the dance?". Instead of just affirming, she got all annoyed with me and wouldn't answer. I really don't know what the guys saw in her. Sure she was pretty enough, but to be honest, she was mean, and acted like she was better than any other female on the planet.

Nevertheless she agreed, and then became famous for not showing up to rehearsal, or showing up late and not caring. She was NEVER there! Poor Suvik never had a partner! Serves him right for picking a girl because he thought she was hot. And when she would come down, she made it clear that she was very tired from her afternoon of never-ending sex. *Classy.* The nights and nights of rehearsal, and doing and redoing, and rechoreographing, and becoming frustrated with the whole thing, and having your feet hurt from the high heels and dancing with a sinus infection (I am so glad that I had

Daniel to catch me on those spins that week even though he was laughing at me), was worth it in the end.

Rehearsing sure was interesting; I don't know how many times I have heard the following words from Tom: "Closer! No Daniel! You want to sleep with her! Not kill her!". We spent months working so hard on this thing, but when it comes down to it, you are in your jeans, in a dirty squash court, on the floor, your partner is probably not wearing shoes – again – and you have to look up at your friend and try and be all seductive while he is circling you like a vulture. Some how we pulled it off. Sometimes, some of us didn't want to go to rehearsal anymore. *No I don't want to look longingly into your eyes tonight, fuck off. I have exams.* And yet we all came, every night at 6:30, religiously, except for of course Bachata, who was tired.

Once we had the dance down, we thought that top hats, high heels and ball gowns were an order, as well as proper shoes for the men, so we wouldn't fall on our faces on International Night. Besides constantly losing the hats and tripping over the skirts, climbing down a dirty metal ladder into a grimy squash court in a ball gown and high heels is not for the faint of heart. One step on the crinoline would be... bad. For me it wasn't just learning that I can choreograph a dance, but loosening up enough to be *in* a dance like that. I had to remember that I wasn't me. I was someone else, someone beautiful, seductive and playful.

The last few weeks of rehearsal, Noah managed to reappear out of hiding and started observing our dance like he was somehow in charge. We invited his opinion, but it was like he was like he was angry about something and wanted credit for a dance he had abandoned months before. A few days later he confronted me in the library.

"So why won't you talk to me anymore?"

I looked up from my binder where I was translating

Egyptian Hieroglyphs - again. "What? I'm not *not* talking to you."

"Yes you are. Whenever I try and say something you act like you are too busy."

"I AM too busy! Hello! I'm learning two languages, writing 3 essays, and single-handedly running International Night!"

He seemed even angrier by this.

"There it is again! You always blame International Night on everything! Just admit you are avoiding me!"

Oh Christ. "Noah you're an idiot."

"Fine, I'm an idiot, but when we broke up I thought we could still be friends!"

Does he want me back or something? What, now that you are out of your little pit of despair you want my company?

"We are still friends... but I am REALLY busy. Like really busy. You can ask any of my friends... I haven't had the time for anything."

He stood up indignantly.

"Sure... Why you need to do this I don't know."

The next few weeks actually got scary. Whenever I saw Noah in the hallway he looked like he was going to punch my face in, especially if I was talking to another guy. He was livid, and frankly unstable. When I went downstairs to do laundry once, which unfortunately was right across from his room, he slammed his door so loud I thought it would break off the hinges. It's so strange that only a few months ago I felt safe around him, and now I was scared. Scared of what he might do. He used to tell me stupid things he did in his youth in anger like breaking windows, and with his revelation of mental instability all I could think was all the various things he could do in a fit of passion. What I couldn't understand is why NOW. Now that he is feeling better, now that he already broke my heart and hid from the world, now he wanted my attention, like nothing happened.

On the bright side, Marie had started to pick up the slack, which made me feel a little guilty for the Kate intrusion. She had each country make a poster and she and I spent one lovely afternoon perusing the Asian market for candleholders. Louise on the other hand was about ready to have half of the hostel drawn and quartered because no one was handing in their recipes on time, and it took hours to recalculate the recipes for 200 people depending on the number of dishes and what ingredients were available in New Zealand.

◙

After my series of harassing rants, threats, and inspiring pep talks to the hostel about getting into their cultural groups and starting rehearsal, I figured that maybe I ought to lead by example and get the North Americans started (there were only 2 Canadians, so we figured we would just group up). At our inaugural meeting nothing happened because no one had any ideas, and I was all idea-ed out from running the damn production, school, and Desert Rose! The main problem was defining exactly what our 'culture' was. You see the problem with North America is that it's sort of world culture now. We have infiltrated the planet!!!! Seriously, there wasn't anything that we could think of that would be characteristically 'North American'. What?! Pioneers? That's just immigration. Coca Cola? Jazz? (We didn't play any instruments and there would already be a Jazz band playing) Rock and Roll music? (Already two rock bands playing and again with the detail of not playing anything) okay... global capitalism? Britney Spears? (If she becomes the symbol of North American culture, I'm immigrating to France).

And then a brilliant idea came to mind. I tossed the notion of showing North American dance throughout the ages, starting at say the 50's, and moving up to now. It counts as North American culture, and could be funny and entertaining. Jenn declared that my idea was THE idea, and it was now our act.

As it turned out, Holly from Texas knew line dancing and thought that we could throw that in as well. The problem was, I was tired. Too tired to harass people for rehearsal, too tired to come up with yet another set of choreography, too tired to do anything more. I left it to everyone else to figure it out. A major problem was getting the American boys to play. Trevor would have, as he can be quite a silly and a gregarious person, but he had broken his foot. None of the other boys would have been caught dead. We were left with Jenn, Holly, and Me. That's it. Everyone else was too cool to join in, and they didn't have any better (or any) ideas. So I got the Kiwis involved. Some even asked me if they could be American. In the end I suppose it was more North American than if it was just those of us with the citizenship because we had people from all over in the dance.

However we never really rehearsed. We had one meeting where Jenn and Holly had put together a compilation of music and we generally figured out what we were going to do. We then had a grand total of three rehearsals where we learned line dancing, and then one complete run through the night before the show. I had no clue what I was doing, but confident I could pull it off if I stayed in the back. It's not that I am a bad dancer; it's just that I didn't want to have a brain freeze in the spotlight. We figured that we could end the number with line dancing, as it is the one dance that has somehow survived, and have everyone in cowboy dress. Except for me, I'd be dressed as an Indian. The day before the show, Rick and Suvik went and bought cap guns from the Two-Dollar shop, and we decided to end our number with those two barrelling-in guns-a-blazin', round everyone up, and have Suvik chuck me over his shoulder kicking and screaming. Nice. Comedy and a cultural statement.

◉

The week before International Night was completely insane. Besides having to study for two language courses I also was burdened with three term papers, not to mention keeping International Night together which was proving to be quite a task. Months before, the hostel committee had decided that if anyone should ruin anything in the music room that it would be locked up for two weeks as penance, for everyone. We had hoped that this would deter another problem and keep the peer pressure up for good behaviour. This was working wonders until Esteban, our in-hostel Mexican, decided to take out his anger on a pair of drumsticks, nearly breaking them in half. Unfortunately this was a week before opening night and the music room was in full use by many groups and holding everyone's instruments. I was not consulted until Frankie sauntered in to the library to inform me that the music room would be locked up and there was nothing I could do about it, International Night was screwed and he didn't care.

"What?!"

"Someone broke a drum stick, we don't know who yet, but it will be locked up. ...You voted on it."

"But we need the music room for rehearsals, International Night is in a week!"

"That's not my problem."

Silence from everyone in the library as they watched the altercation from behind their binders.

"No. It's mine, and I am not letting YOU ruin it for everyone. I have worked too hard on this to be screwed now!"

Ben pipes in from the back "And it's completely unfair mate!"

His tone turned to patronisingly irritated

"You voted on the policy and the *President* of the hostel, *Tomas*, and Doug agree with me. There's nothing you can do. The perpetrator should have thought about their actions before going in there, and everyone will find out and be angry with him. This is the consequence."

"I don't care!" I snarled, "Why am I even talking to you? People are using that room for rehearsal and there is nowhere else to go, and even if there was, their instruments are in there. You are Not locking it up and ruining everything everyone has worked so hard on. I'm talking to Pauline in the morning and having it fixed." Pauline was our Residence Manager.

"Pauline won't do anything, it's our decision."

"You wanna bet." I said as I lowered my voice.

Frankie gave me one last look of defiance before walking out of the room. As the door closed, everyone uttered a sigh and I shouted

"What the Hell!? Is he just trying to screw me over?!?!"

Ben came over and said with a grin.

"Jess that was awesome, I mean I gave my two cents, but you just gave like five dollars! I would not want to mess with you."

Abby looked up from her blue binder.

"Yeah, that was scary mate, I was trying to like, melt through the couch! You really going to talk to Pauline?"

"Yeah, there's no point in talking to anyone else. She'll understand. I hope."

"God, Frankie's such a dick!"

The next morning before class I marched into the office and told Pauline about the problem. Apparently she had already had a visit from Frankie but she agreed that under the circumstances the music room was essential. She decided that since it was Friday, that the room would be kept locked up for the weekend and opened on Monday, however, the hostel would be told it would be closed for the stipulated two weeks to ensure the drum stick breaker would be given as much grief as possible. I felt a little better and told Ben the story, because if anyone needed to know, it was him. He was in four separate acts that involved a full band and was my equipment expert. That, and I figured I owed him a little bit of a break after Marie and Kate chased him around the games room with sparkly blue paintbrushes, cornered him in the music room, while he yelled "AH! Get away from me woman!" in front of a stunned but highly amused Malaysian group who were rehearsing with guitars. They painted his face, and I filmed it with my digital camera.

I seemed to have garnered the title of International Queen at the hostel, and new Asian students that I had never met before were now greeting me in the hallway, like I was someone to greet. The night the music room crisis was solved Jackie and I had decided to run around the hostel and film the hostel and its inhabitants. While we were walking up a stairwell looking for people to bother we ran into a Chinese guy carrying a pizza box. Jackie followed him and started a commentary.

"For the record this is what us IH people have to survive on here because the food is so bloody awful." I laughed, and when the guy stopped, yelled "Ooh! Open the box! Open the box!" He did and both Jackie and I oohed and aahed appropriately before thanking him and turning away. Then he smiled and said,

"Do you want some pizza?"

"What? Are you serious?"

"Yeah."

"Wow! Thank you! Oh my god!"

The camera was still on,

"Wait, wait, just for the record are you actually offering us pizza?"

"Yes, maybe, if you hurry up."

"Wow, thanks matey, you're brilliant!"

"Yeah you rock. Thanks!"

Jackie and I each got a piece and then went on our way, when we were at a safe distance I asked Jackie who he was. She had no idea.

Through all this, Daniel was again being a total shit. He was rude in rehearsal, callous at the dinner table, but in vehement denial over what was going on. He thought that by not saying anything that no one would know. In a residence of 170 students, everyone knows everything. And everyone knew that Daniel and Abby were secretly going out, except it wasn't really a very good secret because everyone knew about it. *Dean and Ayako saw you go in to his room last night, and the entire hallway heard you. We ALL KNOW.* I played dumb until I couldn't stand being lied to anymore. The whole thing was just stupid. I finally confronted him directly about the whole thing.

"So.. Whatcha doing this summer?"

"Oh I dunno, working mostly at the supermarket. Lazing on the beach if I can, you know."

"Won't you be going to Te Kuiti?"

His face went white and his body froze in place. He tried to sound non-chalant

"Why would I go there?"

"Because that's where your girlfriend lives isn't it?"

He stared at me dumbfounded for a minute and stared down at the table. "Yeah."

"Dan did you think I didn't know?"

"I was hoping you didn't" He looked ashamed.

"Why? Who keeps a relationship secret? And everybody knows."

"Well..." Just then Suvik entered the frame and the conversation quickly turned to rugby.

I didn't know if he was ashamed of keeping the relationship a secret from everyone, from me, or if he was ashamed of the relationship itself. On top of all this, Rick was also in the dog-house, what with being non-existent and downright mean to Jackie. Daniel's behaviour could actually be considered "gentlemanly" next to Rick, and Rick was even making Daniel, his best friend, upset with him! It was ridiculous! However mean he could be, he was. It was like he sat in his room at night thinking of nasty things to say. Jackie and I spent many a night sitting on her fluffy zebra printed blanket eating coconut chocolate and spicy instant noodles ranting and consoling before finally deciding that we just didn't care anymore.

Chapter 16

Blur

The day before International Night was even more insane because we weren't allowed to set anything up in the dining hall until after dinner, other than the previous three days that had been set aside for cooking until the wee hours of the morning. We had over 40 different dishes and each group had to have time scheduled to make their meal. I was so thankful that I had nothing to do with that; other than the episode of the infamous apple pies.

You see, Canadian counterpart John, who everyone else knew as "You know, the new Canadian guy? Yeah, the one who never says anything, him." Had refused due to lack of cooking skills to either help or make anything emblematic of our country. Canada had to represent! I decided that the most Canadian food I could make would be apple pie. Of course, once I talked to the chef, I realised that I would need to make 36 apple pies, which involved 108 apples and an obscene amount of flour, sugar, and shortening. Jackie helped me one night to make the pastry, which could easily be refrigerated for a few nights, except, apparently in New Zealand the concept of vegetable shortening is completely foreign, so I was given coconut oil shortening. I figured that it wouldn't make too much of a difference so we went ahead with our giant spoons and excessively deep metal vats making stupid amounts of pastry at midnight, blaring the soundtrack to "Bridget Jones' Diary" in the kitchen.

Fast-forward to the International Night eve and zoom in on me after dinner moving tables for the umpteenth time and waiting for the electricians to arrive while Daniel, Rick, Ben, and John stood staring perplexingly at the ceiling trying to figure out how on earth they would hang the rig they created to hang the backdrop from without damaging the ceiling. Despite Daniel and Rick's bad behaviour the past weeks, they at least put up the backdrop without any sarcasm. Granted they didn't talk to either Jackie or myself except for what was absolutely necessary, but it was an improvement. Daniel, was even bordering on friendship. When Pauline came in to check on our progress the boys volunteered me to ask if they could drill the ceiling, as it was the only way to keep the backdrop up. Since Pauline was leaving at the end of the year for good, and had already let us staple gun the walls with red and black swagged fabric, she agreed. Within minutes, the boys had a big ladder balanced on top of a dinner table and were happily working within violation of every safety code the residence had ever written.

In the meantime, the AV guys had shown up and were about to set up their equipment when we hit a snag. A rather large snag. I had told my contact over the phone that this was a very old residence, built in around the 1960's, and I was unsure what kind of power it had. My contact assured me that there would be no problem and that he would guarantee that they brought all necessary equipment and generators to hook us up. Now there was a plug-in problem. Their stuff needed three-phase power, but the socket that they needed only had one-phase power. The three-phase power was in the kitchen but there was no socket. The one with the long dreadlocks figured that they could just hardwire it into the wall, but they would need to call an electrician to do it.

"Okay, so I'll call round but its not going to be cheap at this time of night."

"Wait, what? This isn't going to cost extra. Your boss told me that everything was fine. I had told him about the power. This isn't my fault."

After much arguing and trying to get Doug to use his fist of RA authority, even though he even admitted that I was boss here, they finally conceded to calling their boss. I had never in my life stood up to two men who clearly knew more about what was going on than I did. I wasn't angry, but I firmly stood my ground and refused to accept anything but the system being set up for the price we had agreed upon. Their boss agreed for an electrician to be called in at 10pm for no charge and everything was put together just fine.

The dining hall was buzzing with so many people that I had to announce unless they were doing something productive, they had to leave. Louise hobbled over carrying the largest box of apples I had ever seen and plunked it on a table.

"What the hell is that?"

"Your apples!"

"Not that many..."

"Yup, 108. Have fun Jess."

"Wait, can you help me peel these?"

"Nope! Nope, you are on your own! I've got Boro-vorse to cook, and Jackie is helping me. Do you know how much meat I have?! Later!"

And she was gone. Luckily Sam came over to start the process of peeling, coring, and chopping 108 apples. Soon, Martin, an acquaintance from another residence, who I had hired to film the show with another student's camera, came over to watch me.

"Damn, girl! You're fast! Can I race you?"

Needless to say I was halfway through my second

apple before he had even finished cutting his first. Sadly, he didn't help after that, and his apple was messy, and part of it had fallen on the floor. As I was slaving away at the apple cart the backdrop boys had put on Guns n' Roses and were now head banging to Paradise City on the table behind the back drop, with only their heads and 'rock on' hands showing.

When I had finished subduing the army of apples, and the AV guys finally left around midnight after their crash course on running their system (everything was hooked up to a master board that had a zillion buttons and switches – their advice: Don't touch anything. Here is the slide to dim the lights.), I moved myself into the kitchen to begin making the 36 apple pies. Unfortunately, when you put coconut shortening into the fridge it gets as hard as a rock and is completely impossible to roll out. *Crap.* I started to put the balls of rock-dough near the stovetop in hopes that it would warm and soften up. This sort of worked, but the amount of pressure and elbow grease I had to use to flatten it out was ridiculous. By 3am I was not even a quarter of the way done and running on pure adrenaline. Jackie looked up from her and Louise's cooking.

"Jess you really need to go to sleep."

"No, I'm not done, I gotta finish."

"Jess, we'll finish it."

With that, Suvik chimed in.

"Yeah I can finish the pies, it's just stuffing them. Go dream of Moose."

"Moose? No no, I have to do it. It's okay."

Then Jackie got that parental look on her face.

"Jess, you have barely slept in nearly a week preparing for tomorrow, and its 3 o'clock in the morning. Suvik and Louise and I will finish your pies. Now, go - to - sleep." I smiled at her.

"No Jaks, it's okay, and besides you still have all that

sausage to cook."

"Do you want me to wake Daniel and have him come and fetch you?"

"What?"

"You know I will, and you know he would, and he'd make you stay in there. So, go now, or I go."

Everyone was staring at me in silence. I looked at Suvik who was already rolling out dough for the next pie.

"I wouldn't argue with her man. It'll be fine. They're still your pies. I'm just assembling."

I was too tired to argue or be able to tell if Jackie was bluffing or not so I played it safe and went to bed.

◉

Apparently Sam came in at around 4:30am to pass out on my floor, but the next morning she was up and bustling about downstairs helping Marie to put the country posters on the windows. With the second bite of my breakfast I had Tom at my table with a sheet detailing the acts and what order they ought to be in and a barrage of questions on how he should handle backstage management, to which I pulled on logic and what I had seen in a high school production of 'Oklahoma!'. A few minutes later Jazmin ran up telling me that rehearsal for the opening number, which I was apparently now in, was in a couple of minutes. And then Jenn and Travis, our two American MC's accosted me in the hallway for approval of their schtick. Seconds later, Tom was back dragging me into Daniel's room for a last minute approval of the music for the party afterwards, which we had all gone over a week before when they used most of my music.

I then remembered that my dress wasn't finished. I ran off to Jackie's room to sew together a North American Indian dress with no pattern on a sewing machine I had borrowed off of Pauline. We discovered that if you sew the material right side out and fringe the edges, it looks pretty good. I borrowed a brown beaded belt and ran back to the dining hall where I found Pauline, who wanted to know every detail of the electrician- hardwir-ing-equipment-into-the-kitchen-wall-escapade, why she hadn't been informed (we couldn't get a hold of her), and if could it be undone. And then sometime after lunch – *I had lunch?* – Martin arrived wanting to know where the camera was and how that was all going to work. I had no idea where the camera was, nor the owner who was M.I.A. With the permission of an R.A., I threw myself at the feet of Diyon, who just happened to have a metal lock pick, which I don't want to know where he got. He a little too swiftly broke into the room and we swiped the cam-era for set up. The other problem is that he didn't get an-other tape like he said he would, so we only had enough time for about two hours. Which was not enough time to film the entire night.

We had a swift Desert Rose rehearsal on the new stage with an angry Daniel because everyone was late, before Ben abducted me off the floor for last minute in-structions on running the lighting and sound. I had to admit that I had no clue what to do as I hadn't seen any of the numbers except for Africa, which I had also helped out in the Drama department, I didn't know what any of the buttons did, and no-one had sent me lighting instruc-tions. I supposed we could put the lights in a generic kind of way unless someone told him otherwise, and to just follow the act list for music, unless it was live, and then to be sure to remind the musicians, to tell him which micro-phone or plug they had so he could turn it on. Then, while I was figuring out what to do for my part in the opening number I ran back up to my room to collect the converted slideshow-video off my computer only to find out that my computer had not only decided not to con-vert it to .mpg format but ate it. I then had a heart attack and died.

***

I came back downstairs white as a ghost just in time for dinner when Martin crossed my path.

"Sweetheart are you okay?"

"uhhuh" He took my shoulders.

"Okay stop. Look at me. LOOK at me. Everything is fine. I've called around and we are looking for a girl I know that has a camera, no one will notice that there is no slideshow. Now breathe. No. Properly. Take a deep breath... without being condescending. Do iiit. There. You okay? Everything will be fine beautiful; just relax. You can't do anything anymore."

I don't think Martin had ever been so nice to me in his life than at that moment. I sat down at the front table with Jackie, Louise, Marie, Sam, and Kate, and then noticed that Daniel and Rick were sitting with Bachata and Abby at the farthest table away from us and ignoring us completely. Jackie got up and invited them to join our table, the "Desert Rose" table, but they refused. Refused and totally ignored us. *Nice.*

Strangely enough, or maybe it was the strange punch the Malaysians made, the night seemed to go without a hitch. Everyone was at their best, and some of the numbers were sensational, others stunk (I am sorry, but HOW is Tai Chi set to low off key singing entertaining?), but most were great. Jenn and Travis had the audience in stitches and the food was beyond fantastic, especially the roasted pig that the Pacific Islanders had cooked on a spit in the parking lot that afternoon. Martin's friend came through, and the only thing missed was Jenn and Travis's little rap, where Jenn made the sound effects and Travis said "UH..... Uh, What?. Yeah. Yeah UH. Word. Uh...." until we had fallen onto the floor and our stomachs hurt from laughing at the complete ridiculousness.

Desert Rose was right after dessert and I was so nervous my stomach was at my feet and I was sitting on the floor with my forehead against the wall because I was certain that I couldn't stand up. Once we got into place, the tension was broken by the music being wrong. Three times. "Didn't you guys know? We're doing our own interpretation of the Indian dance!" Nevertheless, the music started and smoke filled the floor, the first beat and I looked up and then we were off. Spinning, flying through the air, low dips, hand stroking my face, the best shimmy I have ever done, Daniel just going for it, and the cat calls from the audience ("Go DAN!"). I noticed that his leg was shaking as I sat down, he must have been so nervous, but he never faltered. As the dance came to an end and the hat came down for the last note, and his head came in for the implied kiss, his forehead knocked into mine behind the hat. I suppose he got a little too into it. The audience roared and cheered for us. I was SO proud. We had put in so much blood, sweat, and tears, and we prevailed. No, we were epic.

At the end of the night, Jackie took the microphone and, without warning, called me up on stage. She handed me chocolate and announced to everyone that even though all of the International Representatives had put an enormous amount of work into this night, that it was me who really took the lead and that they couldn't do without. Jackie asked our hostel to give me a round of applause. And they did. I was so embarrassed. Embarrassed but also flattered and thankful that someone had noticed; noticed and taken the time to acknowledge me. Never in my entire life had someone singled me out and told me that I was appreciated and fabulous before. I didn't know what to say. In retrospect the gracious thing to do would have been to bring all the reps up and say to the audience that it was a marriage of skills and that I couldn't have made the night what it was without them, but my mind was blank. I said "thank you" and quickly ran back to my seat, embarrassed that I didn't have something better to say.

The final act then came up on stage, calling themselves the United Nations (Germany on guitar, America on base. Malaysia, Taiwan, and Mexico on vocals, New Zealand on drums) and they began the song "Zombie" by the Cranberries, with a talent and professionalism that impressed everyone, and then slid into "Let's Get Retarded" by the Black Eyed Peas while everyone leaped up onto the dance floor for the post night party. Not only was I given a nod during the show, but afterwards so many of my friends, acquaintances, and random Asian people who I had never met before came up to me to tell me what a great job I did and how amazing the night had turned out. Pauline herself said that it was the best International Night in 10 years. Unfortunately, by 1am I was exhausted. The tired stick finally arrived and smacked me over the head with the weeks of stress, work, and no sleep, and I had to bow out early. The party raged until 3.

The next afternoon, two R.A.s found me in the hallway and simultaneously told me that the tech guys were back for their equipment and that I was to hurry down to the dining hall for clean up. I said I would, and then promptly went to Jackie's room where I conveniently hid until everything was already done. There was NO way that after months of preparation that I was going to clean everything up as well. No. Someone else could do that. No-one questioned me on it either. Jackie was more than happy to hide out with me, because unbeknownst to me, last night, she finally broke up with Rick. She was fed up with him ignoring her, being rude, and treating her like she didn't exist, and also for being shamelessly interested in Bachata.

◉

Once the shenanigans of International Night had ended and the exams had started, my friends and I decided, in true university residence fashion, to have a toga party. In the park. Despite our obvious lack of alcohol, more people than we thought came out with white bed sheets dramatically wrapped around them, and then had Phil fixing them properly once they fell off. Why Phil knew how to actually tie a toga was beyond any of us, and yet unsurprising. So we tramped to Albert Park, Jackie's laptop in hand, one lone candle, and stopped at the gazebo for hi-jinks. We played the music as loud as Jackie's laptop could handle and danced and sang along like idiots, taking roman-statuesque pictures of each of us before videoing Jackie and Tom terribly re-enacting a Haki for me, as well as their post-apologies. Alas, soon it started to rain, so we ran back like lunatics waving our bed sheets in the air back to the warmth of the hostel.

That night Jackie, Kate, and I had one of the last sleep-overs we would ever have. Second semester was nearly over and my departure date was starting to become impendingly obvious. Not that we slept. I was exhausted and had a test the next day, but all I could hear were the giggles of the three amigos through the dark, and the occasional bang on the pipe. I was livid. They wouldn't shut up! *I have a test! They know I have a test! I was sleeping here so I wouldn't have to deal with my evil Malaysian neighbour!* I even asked them to be quiet, but it didn't work. All night all I could hear was the banging of pipes and stifled giggles. The next morning I stormed off to breakfast feeling like death only to meet Jackie at the table. She smiled at me and said she was sorry for keeping me up.

"What the hell Jaks, I have a test today."

"I know Jess, but... didn't you hear it?"

"Hear what? All I heard was you guys laughing. And why were you banging on pipes?"

"Oh god you don't know! You probably thought we

were awful! We couldn't sleep either! God. It was Rick and Bachata ALL NIGHT!"

"What?"

"Yeah, the rocking and banging on the wall was loud! I can't believe you didn't hear it. But, oh you would have loved this. When it got faster, we would bang on the pipe that goes through to Bachata's room, and then the rocking would suddenly stop. Then it would start up again. And when it got fast enough again, we'd bang on the pipes!"

"NO!!!!! That's so MEAN! Brilliant! But mean! Are you sure it was Rick up there?"

"Hell yes! Who else would it be? Serves the bastard right. You know he never tried anything with me at all! Not even a kiss! Told me he wanted to "slow down" because he wasn't ready for a physical relationship. Well he's not going slowly now is he? It makes me think that he just wanted to slow down with ME so he could have her. And what a tramp! How long have they been dating? 2 days?"

"You're evil."

"Ohmygod Bachata just came in, and she looks pissed!"

"I bet she is."

"Yup, not ONE orgasm all night."

"Evil."

She threw her head back and laughed. Just then Bachata's head spun round and shot daggers from her eyes.

DO IT AFRAID

Chapter 17

Leaving

It's funny how life sweeps you up in a cyclone and puts you down somewhere different. The end of the year, the end of adventuring and final exams and not sleeping and International Night planning, just appeared one day, very uneventfully and without symphonic accompaniment or scrolling credits that left me with a feeling of emptiness. The hostel seemed to stick together a little more in the closing weeks; with all of us trying to have a last burst of fun and sign each other's books before we parted ways. Unfortunately alcohol mixed with sadness just makes you feel more miserable. I felt like my heart had imploded. I didn't want to leave, but I couldn't stay. No one wanted me to leave, but no one could put me up for a few months. It all had this overwhelming feeling of absolute finality. The adventure was over, and now I had to go home. Except, I wasn't the same girl who left from Pearson Airport anymore. I had been through so much; seen and done so many things that no one back home would understand or relate to. What if no one back home liked me anymore? What if I didn't like them? Now I was outgoing and fun and - now I had courage. Now I was proud of myself and excited about life.

It was such a strange feeling. We gathered in each other's rooms to burn silly amounts of music, signed books, exchanged photos, and tried to pack in as much together time as we all could while trying desperately to pretend that it wasn't over. I packed one suitcase very early, but the last one I couldn't finish at all. Jackie and Kate had to finish it for me at the last minute. All I could do was sit on my bed and stare at my desk with a glassy countenance.

I had my room cleaned for inspection, and the last night I slept in Jackie's room with Kate. We tried to have a last-ever "Bucket-Punch" party, but sadly, alcohol and depression don't mix. Bucket Punch was a drink that Jackie and I created near the beginning of the second semester. It consisted of her plastic purple bucket, and whatever hard liquor and juice we happened to have around. Normally a night of Bucket Punch meant a night of chocolate and laughter, but that last night we mostly sat around with heavy hearts. Louise came that night to say her good byes because she had to leave early, and I was angry. I was angry I had to leave, and angry she had to leave early and angry I didn't know when I would see any of them again.

"Well if you can't wait to say good bye to me tomorrow, that's fine."

"Aw Jess, don't say *that*. You know I have to leave for work in Nelson. I'd stay if I could."

The tears started welling up in my eyes as I nodded 'yes' and hugged good-bye one of the best friends I have ever had and would maybe never see again. I tried so hard not to cry. I imagined a giant glass bottle sucking up wispy gray clouds of emotion, in hopes that my imagined metaphorical cliché would stop my soul from screaming.

My red book of signatures and odes was finished up that morning and Sam came to pick me up. I was to stay with her for one day before my flight. I asked Daniel to help me with my suitcases, and he said he would but he never came. Suvik carried one for me and Sam fetched the other. My heart was breaking and everything inside hurt. I stood in the parking lot trying to smile as Sam and her mom put my suitcases into the car. And then that was it. I had to get into that car, close the door, and leave. Leave forever. I couldn't bear it. I couldn't do it, but I had to. I hugged each of my friends as they gathered on the pavement and tried to keep it together. Struggling desperately to not cry. The last person to hug was Suvik, and in his strong arms I sobbed. I could barely stand up so he held me up and told me it was okay. I didn't want to go home. I didn't want it to be over. When I pulled myself together I held Jackie one last time, told her I loved her, took a deep breath and stepped into the back seat of the car. Sam's mom asked if I was ready and I nodded as I said "just go" through misty eyes. We drove up the hill that I had walked countless times complaining about the steepness of it and various classes and knew that I would never do it again. My face hurt from crying but once we turned onto the highway I couldn't stop again.

When we finally got to Sam's I fell asleep on her bed, while she wrote in my red memories book. Later on, we ate a wonderful dinner, complete with a chocolate cake her little brother made just for me, and a barbeque. We played the Lord of the Rings, and Spiderman on her Xbox and pretended that tomorrow wouldn't come. Jackie and Kate called that night to make sure I was all right and to tell me they loved me, they would always keep in touch, and that I wasn't allowed to not email or call.

That night, I had a dreamless sleep, but woke up feeling surprisingly better and prepared to go home. I felt numb. Sam's Dad drove me to the airport and he joked about traffic and how it would be funny if after all that effort and tears I missed my flight. I forced a short laugh but really, if I had to go home, I wanted to get it over with. Sam wasn't allowed to go very far with me in the airport because of security. She stood behind the blue

barrier, her bright orange t-shirt contrasting its serious-
ness, tears in her eyes, and stayed there until I walked
through the doors. By the time I got onto the airplane I
had a raging headache and really wasn't interested in
talking to the cute doctor that was sitting beside me. The
flight attendant gave me Panadol and I, yet again, fell
asleep for most of the journey. I slept and waited and
played various computer games on the screen in front of
me; and then a funny thing happened. We landed in Los
Angeles but couldn't dock. We drove around for more
than half an hour waiting for a spot. By the time we finally disembarked and ran through the airport to get to
my terminal, my flight had closed and they wouldn't let
me on. I started to cry in front of the young man at the
ticket counter.

"I just want to go home!"

"Don't cry honey, I'll put you on the next flight okay?
Look, this one leaves in 3 hours."

Tears were streaming down my face "Okay."

"Can you just do one thing for me? One?"

"What?"

"Can you smile for me?"

I furrowed my brow and probably looked confused

"Really, I want to see your smile."

I half forced a smile onto my face.

"There, beautiful smile, I thought so. Just head on
down to security and you will be on your flight in no
time. Okay? Smile."

In the end the delay was perfect because security was
insane. They nearly took apart my laptop and the line up
was silly. There were probably three metal/bomb detec-
tors that I had to go through. Besides the first big one
with all the security guards standing around looking
scary, at the top of the escalator there was one, and at the
end of a corridor there was another. *How would I manage
to pick up an explosive between the escalator and the door?* I

called home and left a message of my new arrival time. In the end the flight delay was great. I bought a strawberry-infused lemonade at Starbucks, which they just didn't make the same in New Zealand, and sat enjoying a taste of home while waiting for my flight.

◉

It's strange. All I wanted when I finally left New Zealand was to just get home. But as the plane screamed onto the runway and I saw the gray buildings of Toronto and the dusting of snow. It took every ounce of strength I had to get off that airplane. Toronto felt exactly the same, as if it had been under a time spell and a year had not gone by at all. A gentleman helped me heave my bags onto my cart and I walked towards the sliding doors that lead to the waiting area. Before I even got down the ramp, Mom pushed past the security guard who was telling her she couldn't go any farther, and threw her arms around me. She felt like home. She had gained weight since I had seen her last, and the fibro-mialgia was clearly taking its toll on her body, reminding me of my Nana when she ran up the ramp, but I didn't care. It was Mom. I hugged the Morgans with a grin and laughed when Alex announced: "Hey look! This woman is from the future!" because it was true. And then Mom and I, with her arm wrapped tightly around my waist, her eyes beaming with pride, walked to her old car with my suitcases, waved goodbye to the Morgans and drove home.

Home. What a complicated word. My room was exactly how I left it. White embroidered duvet, white walls, and white and blue netting draped from the ceiling. It looked so innocent, a room for a little princess. The room didn't fit me anymore. It felt like it should though, this was my room, my apartment, my books. But it didn't feel like mine. My suitcases looked foreign and odd leaning up against the wall; an incursion. I carefully unzipped my suitcases and looked at the contents. I really couldn't unpack now. My dog Sam was ecstatic about my return, bouncing and running around the apartment in fast-forward. I felt like I should be really happy but somehow I knew that I never would fit like I did before.

As the weeks past and I slowly put my things away, Mom asked if I would like to redecorate my room for a fresh start, and we began the process of decorating. I went to see old friends, and they were all the same, but I was different. And no one really wanted to hear my stories, they were polite, but behind most of their eyes was a flicker of resentment. Mom was right. New Zealand was *my* experience, *my* adventure, and anyone who hasn't done something like that would not be able to understand or relate to it, and there is no reason that they should. All me talking about my adventures did was make others see what an average year they had in comparison, and that's not fair. But how do you let go? Do you just forget about it?

As Tolkien once wrote: "How do you pick up the strands of an old life?". The answer is, you can't. Ever. Instead, you have to proudly be the person you became, keep the memories alive in your heart, and go on with your life, however it has changed; without regret.

DO IT AFRAID

DO IT AFRAID

About the Author

Jessica Selzer grew up in Toronto, Ontario Canada with a single mother and has been writing since childhood. At the age of 8 she wrote her first story about a brave unicorn named "Fleur".

While studying at the University of Toronto she was accepted to a Study Abroad program to Auckland, New Zealand, which was the foundation for this book. Jessica graduated with an Honours Bachelor of Arts degree with a double major in Classical Civilizations, and Near & Middle Eastern Studies.

She currently resides in the Pacific Northwest with her family.

This is her first book.

To contact her, please email: doitafraid@gmail.com.

DO IT AFRAID

DO IT AFRAID

DO IT AFRAID

DO IT AFRAID

DO IT AFRAID